	Lesson 3	Ch
		• Practise 14 characters following [illegible] order 十、丰、人、八、川、江、三、丁、月、问、回、国、小、水 • Learn to write Chinese numbers 四、五、六、七、九
	• **Conversation:** greet people for the first time • **Character reading:** recognise characters with the radicals 亻and 女 • **Character writing:** introduce people • **Vocabulary extension:** use different terms of address for people	• Practise six characters with the radicals 亻and 女 你、们、他、她、好、姓 • Learn to write seven common words for greetings and introductions 中文、什么、名字、认识、高兴、对不起、请问
	• **Conversation:** exchange personal information about where you live • **Character reading:** recognise characters with the radicals 口 and 日 • **Character writing:** ask questions about where people come from • **Vocabulary extension:** countries	• Practise five characters with the radicals 口 and 日 叫、吗、明、星、是 • Learn to write nine common words for greetings, nationalities and where people live 早上、不、但、哪里、住、北京、在、美国、英国
	• **Conversation:** ask questions about someone's family • **Character reading:** recognise characters with the radicals 宀 and 阝(right) • **Character writing:** write about occupations • **Vocabulary extension:** occupations	• Practise five characters with the radicals 宀 and 阝(right) 家、安、字、都、那 • Learn to write ten common words for family members and jobs 爸、妈、姐、妹、哥、弟、工作、医生、老师、学生
	• **Conversation:** talk about favourite people • **Character reading:** recognise characters with the radicals 土 and 氵 • **Character writing:** describe where people live • **Vocabulary extension:** expressions used to describe people	• Practise six characters with the radicals 土 and 氵 (出生)地、(上)海、漂(亮)、在、法(国)、演(员) • Learn to write six common words for describing people's appearance 高、可爱、帅、酷、年轻、矮
	• **Writing:** ask for addresses and contact numbers • **Character reading:** recognise characters with the radicals 讠and 辶 • **Character writing:** write about contact numbers • **Vocabulary extension:** words and word order of addresses	• Practise five characters with the radicals 讠and 辶 记(者)、谁、这、(发)送、退(出) • Learn to write seven common words for addresses and contact numbers 电话、号码、多少、地址、路、公寓、房间
	• **Vocabulary:** public holidays in China • **Character reading:** recognise characters with the radicals 月 and 扌 • **Character writing:** write about everyday activities • **Vocabulary extension:** days and dates	• Practise four characters with the radicals 月 and 扌 月、(星)期、打、护(士) • Learn to write nine common words for dates and daily activities 今天、几号、吃饭、去、学、做、见面、看书、上班

Lesson 3	Character writing
• **Reading:** understand people's weekly plans • **Character reading:** recognise characters with the radicals 门 and 足 • **Character writing:** plan social activities • **Vocabulary extension:** leisure activities	• Practise four characters with the radicals 门 and 足 跑(步)、(时)间、门、跟 • Learn to write nine common words for time expressions and daily activities 分、刻、半、点、中午、电影、晚、音乐、唱歌
• **Listening:** understand an introduction from a shop assistant • **Character reading:** recognise characters with the radicals 衤 and 贝 • **Character writing:** write about shopping • **Vocabulary extension:** items of clothing	• Practise eight characters with the radicals 衤 and 贝 裙、裤、衬衫、(售)货员、贵、购 • Learn to write eight common words for clothes, colours and places 衣服、鞋、红、黑、蓝、白、超市、店
• **Reading:** understand descriptions of weekend activities • **Character reading:** recognise characters with the radicals 木 and 彳 • **Character writing:** give directions • **Vocabulary extension:** places in the neighbourhood	• Practise five characters with the radicals 木 and 彳 很、(银)行、往、楼、(手)机 • Learn to write nine common words for directions and types of student housing 东边、南、西、北、前、后、附近、房、宿舍
• **Conversation and listening:** understand dinner plans • **Character reading:** recognise characters with the radicals 又 and 饣 • **Character writing:** make appointments • **Vocabulary extension:** places related to transport	• Practise seven characters with the radicals 又 and 饣 (喜)欢、(头)发、对、(朋)友、双、饭馆 • Learn to write six common words for modes of transport and holiday activities 火车、旅行、爬山、参观、拍照、船
• **Conversation:** talk about a recreational class • **Character reading:** recognise characters with the radicals 王 and 钅 • **Character writing:** describe recreational activities • **Vocabulary extension:** different types of sport	• Practise six characters with the radicals 王 and 钅 玩、现(在)、班、(足)球、钱、(地)铁 • Learn to write six common words for abilities and types of sport 可以、会、游泳、网球、踢、乒乓
• **Conversation and listening:** talk about travel experiences • **Character reading:** recognise characters with the radicals ⺮ and 禾 • **Character writing:** make plans for recreational activities • **Vocabulary extension:** holiday activities	• Practise five characters with the radicals ⺮ and 禾 (打)算、篮(球)、和、租、香(港) • Learn to write six common words for places and holiday activities 地方、城市、西安、好玩、历史、主意

Getting started
Experiencing Chinese

LESSON | 1

Objectives

1 **Pinyin:** identify initials
2 **Pinyin:** identify finals
3 **Pronunciation and listening:** identify the four tones
4 **Pronunciation and listening:** identify the neutral tone
5 **Vocabulary and pronunciation:** Chinese numbers 1 to 10 and their tones
6 **Vocabulary and pronunciation:** Chinese numbers 1 to 10 and their pinyin
7 **Conversation:** common expressions

Pinyin

1 Circle the initials of the pinyin syllables.

1	tā	7	wén
2	de	8	zì
3	lǐ	9	zhōng
4	miàn	10	huá
5	cái	11	kàn
6	néng	12	shū

2 Circle the finals of the pinyin syllables.

1	lǜ	6	xī
2	sè	7	xiàn
3	hǎo	8	zuò
4	rén	9	fàn
5	dōng	10	guǎn

Pronunciation and listening

2

3 Listen and circle the characters with the same tones.

1	ni 你	jiu 九	qi 七
2	wu 五	si 四	er 二
3	ren 人	mei 没	wo 我
4	xie 谢	san 三	wen 问
5	yi 医	yuan 院	sheng 生
6	er 儿	ying 英	xue 学
7	qing 请	bei 贝	hao 好
8	ma 妈	shi 师	dui 对

Now listen again and add tones to the pinyin syllables.

3

4 **Listen and circle the characters with the neutral tone.**

1 shenme 什么

2 hao ma 好 吗

3 baba 爸爸

4 mama 妈妈

5 ni ne 你 呢

6 nanbian 南边

Now listen again and add tones to the pinyin syllables.

Vocabulary and pronunciation

5 **Match the Chinese numbers with the English ones.**

1 二	a one
2 五	b two
3 七	c three
4 八	d four
5 三	e five
6 九	f six
7 四	g seven
8 一	h eight
9 十	i nine
10 六	j ten

Now complete the table with the Chinese numbers.

Tones	Chinese numbers
1st tone	
2nd tone	
3rd tone	
4th tone	

4

6 **Write down the numbers you hear in figures.**

1 ________ ________________

2 ________ ________________

3 ________ ________________

4 ________ ________________

5 ________ ________________

6 ________ ________________

Now listen again and write pinyin for each number, including the correct tone.

Conversation

7 **Complete the conversations with the expressions in the box.**

bú kèqi 不客气	méi guānxi 没关系	zàijiàn 再见

1 A: Zàijiàn 再见！

B: ________________！

2 A: Xièxie 谢谢！

B: ________________。

3 A: Duìbuqǐ 对不起。

B: ________________。

LESSON 2

Objectives

1 **Character reading:** recognise basic Chinese characters
2 **Character reading:** recognise radicals in Chinese characters
3 **Character writing:** the basic strokes
4 **Character writing:** the seven rules of stroke order

Character reading

1 Match the characters with the possible meanings.

1  口 — a sky

2  上 — b mouth

3  下 — c big

4  中 — d up

5  人 — e middle

6  大 — f down

7  天 — g person

2 Identify the radicals of the characters.

1 lín 林	a crowd
2 sēn 森	b burn
3 zhòng 众	c woods
4 cóng 从	d flame
5 fén 焚	e forest
6 yán 炎	f follow
7 míng 明	g friend
8 péng 朋	h bright

Now match the characters with the possible meanings.

Character writing

3 Identify the basic strokes in the characters.

1 六	4 人
2 三	5 八
3 中	6 打

4 Match the characters with the correct stroke orders.

1 十	a from outside to inside, then closing
2 人	b from left to right
3 川	c horizontal before vertical
4 丁	d middle before two sides
5 问	e downward left before downward right
6 回	f from top to bottom
7 小	g from outside to inside

CHARACTER WRITING

Objectives

1 Practise 14 characters following the seven rules of stroke order

2 Learn to write Chinese numbers

1 Write the characters following the correct stroke order.

1 horizontal before vertical

shí *ten*

十

fēng *rich*

丰

2 downward left before downward right

rén *people*

人

bā *eight*

八

3 from left to right

chuān *river*

川

jiāng *big river*

江

4 from top to bottom

sān *three*

三

dīng *a Chinese surname*

丁

5 from outside to inside

yuè *moon, month*

月

wèn *ask*

问 问 问 问 问 问

问

6 from outside to inside, then closing

huí *return*

回 回 回 回 回 回

回

guó *country*

国 国 国 国 国 国 国 国

国

7 middle before two sides

xiǎo *small*

小 小 小

小

shuǐ *water*

水 水 水 水

水

2 Write the characters following the correct stroke order.

sì *four*

四 四 四 四 四

四

wǔ *five*

五 五 五 五

五

liù *six*

六 六 六 六

六

qī *seven*

七 七

七

jiǔ *nine*

九 九

九

UNIT 1 你好！(Nǐ hǎo) Hello!

LESSON 1

Objectives

1 **Vocabulary:** greetings and introductions
2 **Listening:** identify people's names and the four tones
3 **Pronunciation:** the four tones
4 **Grammar:** identify surnames and given names
5 **Conversation and listening:** understand greetings and introductions

Vocabulary

1 Match the words with the meanings.

1	名字	a	get to know
2	什么	b	glad, happy
3	认识	c	name
4	高兴	d	what
5	请问	e	may I ask, excuse me

Listening

5

2 Listen and check the names you hear.

1 ☐ a 丁 辉 (Dīng Huī) ☐ b 丁 慧 (Dīng Huì)
2 ☐ a 王 丽雅 (Wáng Lìyǎ) ☐ b 王 丽娅 (Wáng Lìyà)
3 ☐ a 淑英 (Shūyīng) ☐ b 淑婷 (Shūtíng)
4 ☐ a 张 仪 (Zhāng Yí) ☐ b 张 毅 (Zhāng Yì)

Pronunciation

3 Circle the correct tones for the characters.

1 我
wō wó wǒ wò

2 什
shēn shén shěn shèn

3 叫
jiāo jiáo jiǎo jiào

4 名
mīng míng mǐng mìng

5 姓
xīng xíng xǐng xìng

Now write pinyin for the words.

6 你好 ________________
7 请问 ________________
8 什么 ________________
9 名字 ________________
10 你呢 ________________
11 认识 ________________
12 高兴 ________________
13 对不起 ________________

Grammar

4 Complete the sentences with the correct parts of people's names.

Wǒ shì Dīng Gāo' ān
1 我是丁 高安。

Wǒ xìng míngzi jiào
我姓________，名字叫________。

Tā shì Wáng Yúnmíng
2 他是王 云明。

Tā xìng míngzi jiào
他姓________，名字叫________。

Wǒ shì Lǐ Wěi
3 我是李伟。

Wǒ xìng wǒ jiào
我姓________，我叫________。

Tā shì Sòng Yùxīng
4 她是宋 玉兴。

Tā xìng míngzi jiào
她姓________，名字叫________。

Wǒ shì Lín Mǎkè
5 我是林马克。

Wǒ xìng wǒ jiào
我姓________，我叫________。

Tā shì Liú Lì
6 她是刘丽。

Tā xìng tā jiào
她姓________，她叫________。

Tā shì Zhāng Wěi
7 他是张伟。

Tā xìng tā jiào
他姓________，他叫________。

Conversation and listening

5 Complete the conversation.

永民：你好！

安娜：(1) ____________！

永民：请问，你叫什么名字？

安娜：(2) ____________ 安娜。你呢？

永民：我叫永民，Kim Yeong-min。

(3) ____________ 你很高兴，

安小姐。

安娜：(4) ____________，我姓Pollard。

6 **Now listen and check the true statements.**

☐ 5 Anna and Yeong-min are meeting for the first time.

☐ 6 Yeong-min's given name is Kim.

☐ 7 Yeong-min knows Anna's family name.

☐ 8 People often say 认识你很高兴 when they meet for the first time.

☐ 9 People often say 对不起 when they meet for the first time.

LESSON | 2

Objectives

1 **Reading:** recognise different kinds of name
2 **Writing:** create an introduction
3 **Writing:** introduce someone
4 **Grammar:** word order of Chinese sentences (I)
5 **Grammar:** verbs 叫, 姓 and 是
6 **Grammar:** questions ending with 呢

Reading

7

1 Read Yeong-min's introduction and answer the questions.

大家好！
我叫Kim Yeong-min，
中文名字是永民。
认识你们很高兴。

1 他姓什么？

____

2 他叫什么名字？

____

3 他的中文名字是什么？

____

Writing

8

2 Read James' self-introduction and write a response.

你好！我叫 James Whitbread，中文名字是詹姆斯。认识你很高兴。

____

____

____

____

____

____

3 Write a few sentences about a friend using 叫, 姓 and 是.

Tā Tā jiào
他 / 她 叫 ____________________

____

____

____

____

____

Grammar

4 Put the words in the correct order to make sentences.

jiào / Wáng Yù / wǒ
1 叫 / 王 玉 / 我 / 。

____

Ānnà / shì / tā
2 安娜 / 是 / 她 / 。

____

tā / míngzi / shénme / jiào
3 他 / 名字 / 什么 / 叫 / ?

____

Zhōngwén míngzi / Mǎkè / shì / de
4 中文 名字 / 马克 / 是 / Mark 的 / 。

____

shénme / xìng / nǐ
5 什么 / 姓 / 你 / ?

____

xìng / Wáng / wǒ
6 姓 / 王 / 我 / 。

____

5 Complete the conversations with the words in the box.

jiào 叫	xìng 姓	shì 是

王玉： 你们好, 我 (1) __________ 王, (2) __________ 王玉, 认识你们很高兴。

永民： 你们好! 我 (3) __________ Kim Yeong-min, 中文名字 (4) __________ 永民。你 (5) __________什么名字?

6 Match the questions with the answers.

Wǒ xìng Wáng nǐ ne
1 我 姓 王 ， 你 呢? ____

Wǒ jiào Ānnà nǐ ne
2 我 叫 安娜, 你 呢? ____

Wǒ shì Shǐdìfū nǐ ne
3 我 是 史蒂夫, 你 呢? ____

Wǒ xìng nǐ ne
4 我 姓 Pollard, 你 呢? ____

Wǒ jiào nǐ ne
5 我 叫 Angela, 你 呢? ____

Wǒ shì nǐ ne
6 我 是 Steve, 你 呢? ____

Wǒ jiào Yǒngmín hěn gāoxìng rènshi nǐ
a 我 叫 永民 ， 很 高兴 认识 你。

Wǒ shì Wáng Yù
b 我 是 王 玉。

Wáng xiān sheng nǐ hǎo wǒ xìng Liú
c 王 先 生 ， 你 好, 我 姓 刘。

Wǒ xìng
d 我 姓 Smith。

nǐ hǎo wǒ shì
e Steve, 你 好, 我 是 Michael。

Nǐ hǎo Wǒ jiào
f 你 好 , Angela, 我 叫 Mark。

LESSON 3

Objectives

1 **Conversation:** greet people for the first time

2 **Character reading:** recognise characters with the radicals 亻 and 女

3 **Character writing:** introduce people

4 **Vocabulary extension:** use different terms of address for people

Conversation

1 Put the sentences in the correct order to make a conversation.

a 我叫李华。认识你很高兴，刘小姐。

b 我叫刘丽。你呢？

c 认识你很高兴。

d 你好！请问，你叫什么名字？

The correct order is ______________________.

Character reading

2 Match the radicals with the meanings.

1 亻	a woman
2 女	b man, person

Now match the words with the meanings.

3 她	c they
4 小姐	d Miss
5 伟	e she, her
6 他们	f great

Character writing

3 Make sentences using the words given.

1 她 小姐

____

2 他 伟

____

Vocabulary extension

4 Complete the sentences with the words in the box.

xiānsheng 先生	xiǎojiě 小姐	nǚshì 女士
tàitai 太太	lǎoshī 老师	tóngxué 同学

1 Ding Yuan is a teacher. You address him as ______________.

2 Mark, Anna and Steve are schoolmates. They call each other ______________.

3 You address Wang Yu, a young woman, as ______________.

4 You meet Mr Wang. You greet and address him as ______________.

5 You meet Mr Wang's wife on the street. You address her as ______________.

6 You see a middle-aged man on campus and want to ask him the way to the student dormitory. You address him as ______________.

7 You meet a young girl at the dining hall in a university. You call her ______________.

8 You address a middle-aged woman at a conference as ______________.

CHARACTER WRITING

Objectives

1 Practise six characters with the radicals 亻 and 女

2 Learn to write seven common words for greetings and introductions

1 Write the characters with the radicals 亻 and 女.

nǐmen *you (plural)*

你 你 你 你 你 你 你

们 们 们 们 们

tā *he, him*

他 他 他 他 他

tā *she, her*

她 她 她 她 她 她

hǎo *good*

好 好 好 好 好 好

xìng *surname*

姓 姓 姓 姓 姓 姓 姓 姓

2 Write the words following the correct stroke order.

Zhōngwén *Chinese*

中 中 中 中

文 文 文 文

shénme *what*

什 什 什 什

么 么 么

míngzi *name*

名 名 名 名 名 名

名

字 字 字 字 字 字

字

rènshi *know, get to know*

认 认 认 认

认

识 识 识 识 识 识

识

识

gāoxìng *glad, happy*

高 高 高 高 高 高

高 高 高 高

高

兴 兴 兴 兴 兴 兴

兴

duìbuqǐ *sorry*

对 对 对 对 对

对

不 不 不 不

不

起 起 起 起 起 起

起 起 起 起

起

qǐngwèn *may I ask*

请 请 请 请 请 请

请 请 请 请

请

问 问 问 问 问 问

问

SELF-ASSESSMENT

Complete the checklist, using the criteria below.

1 = I need a lot of help to do this.
2 = I can do this with a little help.
3 = I can do this fairly well.
4 = I can do this very well.
5 = I can do this almost perfectly.

LANGUAGE SKILL	PROGRESS	YOUR SCORE
PRONUNCIATION	• I can identify the four tones. • I can say common Chinese surnames with the correct tones.	
VOCABULARY	• I know at least three Chinese surnames. • I know common words and expressions used to greet people. • I know common words and phrases used to introduce myself and other people.	
GRAMMAR	• I can identify the surname and given name of a Chinese person. • I understand basic word order in Chinese sentences. • I know how to use the verbs 叫, 姓 and 是 to talk about people's names. • I can ask questions about people's names using 什么. • I can ask follow-up questions with 呢.	
LISTENING	• I can identify people's names. • I can understand simple greetings and introductions.	
READING	• I know the meanings of the radicals 亻 and 女. • I can understand people's simple self-introductions.	
SPEAKING	• I can introduce myself and my friends. • I can ask for people's names.	
WRITING	• I can write six characters with the radicals 亻 and 女, and seven common words for greetings and introductions. • I can write a basic self-introduction.	

UNIT 2 你是哪国人？

Nǐ shì nǎ guó rén

Which country are you from?

LESSON | 1

Objectives

1 **Vocabulary:** words used to talk about nationalities

2 **Vocabulary:** country names

3 **Conversation and listening:** identify someone's nationality, where they come from and where they live

4 **Listening:** identify where people come from

5 **Pronunciation:** the four tones

6 **Grammar:** yes/no questions ending with 吗

Vocabulary

1 Match the words with the meanings.

1 住在 (zhù zài)	a no
2 哪国 (nǎ guó)	b where
3 不 (bù)	c people
4 人 (rén)	d which country
5 吗 (ma)	e live at/in
6 哪里 (nǎli)	f particle used to ask questions

2 Match the country names with the pictures.

1 英国 (Yīngguó) ______	5 加拿大 (Jiānádà) ______
2 澳大利亚 (Àodàlìyà) ______	6 中国 (Zhōngguó) ______
3 美国 (Měiguó) ______	7 法国 (Fǎguó) ______
4 日本 (Rìběn) ______	8 韩国 (Hánguó) ______

a

b

c

d

e

f

g

h

Conversation and listening

9

3 Listen to the conversation and complete the sentences.

马克：你们好，我是马克。
你叫什么名字？

王玉：你好，我叫王玉。他是史蒂夫。

马克：史蒂夫，你是哪国人？

史蒂夫：我是英国人。你呢？

马克：我是澳大利亚人。

史蒂夫：你住在悉尼吗？

马克：不，我住在北京。

1 史蒂夫是 ____________ 人。

2 马克是 ____________ 人。

3 马克住在 ____________。

Listening

10

4 Listen and check where the speakers are from.

1 ☐ a 韩国 ☐ b 日本

2 ☐ a 澳大利亚 ☐ b 加拿大

3 ☐ a 美国 ☐ b 英国

4 ☐ a 法国 ☐ b 中国

Pronunciation

5 Write pinyin for the words.

1 英国 ____________

2 伦敦 ____________

3 中国 ____________

4 北京 ____________

5 日本人 ____________

6 澳大利亚人 ____________

Grammar

6 Ask questions about the sentences using 吗.

1 ____________

Wáng Yù shì Zhōngguórén
王玉是中国人。

2 ____________

Wǒ zhù zài Běijīng
我住在北京。

3 ____________

Yǒngmín shì Hánguórén
永民是韩国人。

4 ____________

Wǒ bú rènshi Dīng Yuán
我不认识丁原。

5 ____________

Mǎkè zhù zài Běijīng
马克住在北京。

LESSON | 2

Objectives

1 **Reading:** people's nationalities and where they live
2 **Reading:** identify a person's nationality
3 **Writing:** describe where someone comes from and where they live
4 **Grammar:** questions with an interrogative pronoun 哪里 and 哪国
5 **Grammar:** negative adverb 不
6 **Conversation:** talk about nationalities

Reading

11

1 Read these people's name cards.

Peter Austin
美国人
住在澳大利亚悉尼

Kim Park
韩国人
住在中国北京

Jane Lee
加拿大人
住在日本

Now answer the questions.

1 Peter 姓什么?

____

2 Peter 是澳大利亚人吗?

____

3 Kim 是中国人吗?

____

4 Kim 住在哪里?

____

5 Jane 是哪国人?

____

6 Jane 住在日本吗?

____

12

2 Read the introduction and answer the questions.

Jackie Chan 是好莱坞明星。但是他不是美国人，他是中国人。

1 Jackie Chan 是明星吗?

____

2 他是哪国人?

____

Writing

3 **Write three sentences to introduce Steve.**

____

____

____

____

Grammar

4 **Ask questions about the underlined parts of the sentences using 哪里 or 哪国.**

Wǒ zhù zài Běijīng
1 我 住 在 <u>北京</u>。

____

Tā zhù zài Lúndūn
2 他 住 在 <u>伦敦</u>。

____

Shǐdìfū shì Yīngguórén
3 史蒂夫 是 <u>英国</u>人 。

____

Tā shì Rìběnrén
4 她 是 <u>日本</u>人。

____

5 **Put 不 in the correct places in the sentences.**

Lúndūn zài Měiguó
1 伦敦 在 美国。

____

Tā jiào Mǎ Lì
2 她 叫 马 丽。

____

Wǒ rènshi Ānnà
3 我 认识 安娜。

____

Now answer the questions using your own information, and using 不 when necessary.

Nǐ zhù zài Běijīng ma
4 你 住 在 北京 吗？

____

Nǐ shì Yīngguórén ma
5 你 是 英国人 吗？

____

Conversation

6 **Complete the conversations using the correct words in the brackets.**

Wáng Yù shì nǎguó zhù zài rén
1 A: 王 玉 是 ________ (哪 国 / 住 在) 人？

Tā shì Zhōngguórén Zhōngguó
B: 她 是 ________ (中国人 / 中国)。

Tāmen shì nǎ guó rén Měiguó
2 A: 他们 是 ________ (哪 国 人 / 美国)？

Duìbuqǐ Nǐ hǎo wǒ bù zhīdào
B: ________ (对不起 / 你 好)，我 不 知道 。

Mǎkè shì Yīngguórén ma
3 A: 马克 是 英国人 吗？

Tā shì jiào Yīngguórén
B: 他 ________ (是 / 叫) 英国人 。

LESSON 3

Objectives

1 **Conversation:** exchange personal information about where you live
2 **Character reading:** recognise characters with the radicals 口 and 日
3 **Character writing:** ask questions about where people come from
4 **Vocabulary extension:** countries

Conversation

1 Complete the conversation with the words in the box.

nǎ guó rén 哪 国 人	zhù zài 住 在	Lúndūn 伦敦
nǐ hǎo 你 好	Yīngguórén 英国人	Běijīng 北京

丁云：你好！我叫丁云。我是中国人，住在 (1) __________。

史蒂夫：丁云，(2) __________！我叫史蒂夫。

丁云：请问，你是 (3) __________？

史蒂夫：我是 (4) __________。

丁云：你住在 (5) __________ 吗？

史蒂夫：不，我 (6) __________ 北京。

Character reading

2 Match the radicals with the meanings.

1 口   a sun

2 日   b mouth

Now match the words with the meanings.

3 呢   c bright

4 是   d be

5 哪   e particle used to ask questions

6 明   f which

Character writing

3 Make questions using the words given.

1 日本人   吗

____

2 是   哪国

____

Vocabulary extension

4 Complete the table with the countries in the box.

a Yīngguó 英国	f Fǎguó 法国	k Déguó 德国
b Měiguó 美国	g Jiānádà 加拿大	l Mòxīgē 墨西哥
c Nánfēi 南非	h Kěnníyà 肯尼亚	m Āijí 埃及
d Zhōngguó 中国	i Rìběn 日本	n Hánguó 韩国
e Xīnjiāpō 新加坡	j Tàiguó 泰国	o Yìndù 印度

Continent	Countries
Asia	
Europe	
America	
Africa	

CHARACTER WRITING

Objectives

1 Practise five characters with the radicals 口 and 日

2 Learn to write nine common words for greetings, nationalities and where people live

1 Write the characters with the radicals 口 and 日.

jiào *be called*

叫

ma *particle used to ask questions*

吗

míngxīng *celebrity*

明

星

shì *be*

是

2 Write the words following the correct stroke order.

zǎoshang *morning*

早

上

bù *no*

不

dàn *but*

但

nǎli *where*

哪

里

zhù *live*

住

Běijīng *Beijing*

北

京

zài *at, in*

在

Měiguó *US*

美

国

Yīngguó *UK*

英

国

SELF-ASSESSMENT

Complete the checklist, using the criteria below.

1 = I need a lot of help to do this.
2 = I can do this with a little help.
3 = I can do this fairly well.
4 = I can do this really well.
5 = I can do this almost perfectly.

LANGUAGE SKILL	PROGRESS	YOUR SCORE
PRONUNCIATION	• I can identify the four tones. • I can say country names with the correct tones.	
VOCABULARY	• I can name at least six countries. • I can name at least four cities. • I know common words and phrases used to tell people my nationality and where I live. • I know how to introduce someone's nationality, where they are from, and where they live.	
GRAMMAR	• I can ask yes/no questions with 吗. • I can ask questions about places and nationalities using 哪里 and 哪国. • I can make negative sentences with 不.	
LISTENING	• I can identify people's nationality. • I can understand people saying where they are from. • I can understand people saying where they live.	
READING	• I know the meanings of the radicals 口 and 日. • I can recognise characters to understand people's self-introductions, including nationality and where they live.	
SPEAKING	• I can introduce my nationality and other people's. • I can ask people where they are from and where they live.	
WRITING	• I can write five characters with the radicals 口 and 日, and nine common words for nationalities and where people live. • I can write a short passage introducing someone's nationality and where they live.	

UNIT 3 你做什么工作？
Nǐ zuò shénme gōngzuò

What do you do?

LESSON 1

Objectives

1 **Vocabulary:** occupations and family members

2 **Vocabulary:** words used to talk about occupations

3 **Conversation and listening:** identify information about family members and their occupations

4 **Reading and writing:** identify information about family members and write about one's own family

5 **Pronunciation:** the finals: a, e, i

Vocabulary

1 Circle the odd word out in each line.

1	bàba 爸爸	jìzhě 记者	māma 妈妈
2	gōngzuò 工作	dìdi 弟弟	jiějie 姐姐
3	yīshēng 医生	hùshi 护士	yīyuàn 医院
4	míngxīng 明星	xuéshēng 学生	lǎoshī 老师

2 Translate the words into Chinese.

1 do __________

2 work, job __________

3 what __________

4 where __________

Conversation and listening

3 Complete the conversation with the words in the box.

xuéshēng 学生	jiějie 姐姐	yīyuàn 医院
nǎli 哪里	zhàopiàn 照片	gōngzuò 工作

马克：你好，刘丽。

刘丽：你好，马克。这是我家的 (1) __________。

马克：刘丽，她是你姐姐吗？

刘丽：是，她是我 (2) __________。

马克：她住在 (3) __________？

刘丽：她住在悉尼。

马克：我弟弟也住在悉尼。你姐姐在哪里 (4) __________？

刘丽：她在 (5) __________ 工作，她是医生。你弟弟呢？

马克：他是 (6) __________。

13 Now listen to the conversation and check the true statements.

☐ 7 刘丽和马克都是医生。

☐ 8 马克的弟弟和刘丽的姐姐都住在悉尼。

☐ 9 刘丽的姐姐在医院工作。

☐ 10 马克的弟弟不是学生。

Reading and writing

14 **4** Read the excerpt from Mark's letter about his family and check the true statements.

> 我爸爸是医生，我妈妈也是医生，他们都在医院工作。我妹妹是记者，我弟弟是学生。

☐ 1 马克的爸爸在医院工作。

☐ 2 马克的妈妈不是医生。

☐ 3 马克的妹妹是学生。

☐ 4 马克的弟弟不是记者。

Now write three sentences about your own family.

5 ______________________

6 ______________________

7 ______________________

Pronunciation

5 Write pinyin for the words.

1 他 ______________________

2 爸爸 ______________________

3 妈妈 ______________________

4 哪 ______________________

5 加拿大 ______________________

6 法国 ______________________

7 也 ______________________

8 这 ______________________

9 和 ______________________

10 哥哥 ______________________

11 记者 ______________________

12 呢 ______________________

13 一 ______________________

14 弟弟 ______________________

15 是 ______________________

16 名字 ______________________

17 哪里 ______________________

18 医生 ______________________

LESSON 2

Objectives

1 **Reading:** understand an introduction to someone's family
2 **Writing:** introduce someone's family
3 **Grammar:** adverbs 也 and 都
4 **Grammar:** word order of Chinese sentences (II)
5 **Grammar:** pronouns as modifiers + 的

Reading

15

1 Read Ding Yun's introduction and answer the questions.

我叫丁云，我是学校的老师。学生都叫我丁老师。我哥哥也是老师，他在英国。我姐姐在法国，她是记者。

1 丁云做什么工作？

______

2 他在哪里工作？

______

3 他哥哥住在哪里？他姐姐呢？

______

Writing

2 Write four sentences about your best friend's family.

______

______

______

______

Grammar

3 Put 也 and 都 in the correct places in the sentences.

Mǎkè hé Yǒngmín bú rènshi Ānnà
1 马克和 永民 不认识安娜。

Tā hěn gāoxìng wǒ hěn gāoxìng
2 他很 高兴， 我很 高兴。

Wǒ bàba māma shì yīshēng
3 我爸爸妈妈是 医生 。

Wǒ dìdi zhù zài Běijīng
4 我弟弟住在北京。

Tā xìng Dīng wǒ xìng Dīng
5 他姓 丁，我姓 丁。

Wǒ shì xuésheng wǒ mèimei shì xuésheng
6 我是 学生 ，我妹妹是 学生。

Tāmen shì xuéxiào de lǎoshī
7 他们是 学校 的老师。

Shǐdìfū shì Yīngguórén
8 史蒂夫是 英国人。

Now check the correct sentences.

Tā jiào Mǎkè tā bàba dōu jiào Mǎkè
☐ 9 他叫马克，他爸爸都叫马克。

Wáng Yù hé Wáng Yún dōu xìng Wáng
☐ 10 王玉和王云都姓王。

Yīshēng hé hùshi yě zài yīyuàn gōngzuò
☐ 11 医生和护士也在医院 工作 。

Wǒ gēge hé dìdi dōu bú zhù zài Běijīng
☐ 12 我哥哥和弟弟都不住在北京。

4 Put the words in the correct order to make sentences.

zài yīyuàn gōngzuò tā
1 在 医院 / 工作 / 她 / 。

____

Yǒngmín Hánguórén shì yě
2 永民 / 韩国人 / 是 / 也 /。

____

Běijīng Wáng Yù zhù zài
3 北京 / 王 玉 / 住 在 /。

____

Zhōngwén míngzi de Ānnà shì
4 中文 名字 / 的 / 安娜 / 是 / Anna /。

____

dōu xuéshēng shì wǒmen
5 都 / 学生 / 是 / 我们 /。

____

Xīní zhù zài bú Mǎkè
6 悉尼 / 住 在 / 不 / 马克 /。

____

yě Běijīng wǒ zhù zài
7 也 / 北京 / 我 / 住 在 /。

____

zài xuéxiào gōngzuò tā gēge
8 在 / 学校 / 工作 / 她 哥哥 /。

____

Now write two sentences about yourself using 也 and 都.

9 ______________________________

10 ______________________________

5 Put the words in the correct order to make noun phrases.

gōngzuò yīshēng de
1 工作 / 医生 / 的

____

xuéshēng wǒ de
2 学生 / 我 / 的

____

zhàopiàn Ānnà jiā de
3 照片 / 安娜 / 家 / 的

____

hùshi yīyuàn de
4 护士 / 医院 / 的

____

gōngzuò bàba de
5 工作 / 爸爸 / 的

____

zhàopiàn jiějie de
6 照片 / 姐姐 / 的

____

Now check the correct sentences.

Wǒ māma zài yīyuàn gōngzuò
☐ 7 我 妈妈 在 医院 工作。

Wǒ míngzi shì Wáng Yù
☐ 8 我 名字 是 王 玉。

Zhè shì wǒ de jiā de zhàopiàn
☐ 9 这 是 我 的 家 的 照片。

Wǒ jiějie shì yīyuàn de hùshi
☐ 10 我 姐姐 是 医院 的 护士。

LESSON 3

Objectives

1 **Conversation:** ask questions about someone's family

2 **Character reading:** recognise characters with the radicals 宀 and 阝(right)

3 **Character writing:** write about occupations

4 **Vocabulary extension:** occupations

Conversation

1 **Write questions for the answers to complete the conversation.**

A: ______________________________?

B: 我叫刘瑜。

A: ______________________________?

B: 我爸爸叫刘伟。

A: ______________________________?

B: 他是中国人。

A: ______________________________?

B: 我妈妈也是中国人。

A: ______________________________?

B: 他们都住在北京。

Character reading

2 **Match the radicals with the meanings.**

1 宀 **a** city

2 阝(right) **b** roof

Now match the words with the meanings.

3 安 **c** that

4 那 **d** both, all

5 家 **e** family, home

6 都 **f** safe and stable

Character writing

3 **Make sentences using the words given.**

1 都 医生

____

2 哪里 工作

____

Vocabulary extension

4 **Complete the table with the words in the box.**

dǎoyóu 导游	lǜshī 律师	chúshī 厨师
mìshū 秘书	gōngchéngshī 工程师	fúwùyuán 服务员
hùshi 护士	lǐfàshī 理发师	xiūlǐgōng 修理工

工作地点（place）	职业（job）
室内（indoors）	
室外（outdoors）	

CHARACTER WRITING

Objectives

1 Practise five characters with the radicals 宀 and 阝(right)

2 Learn to write ten common words for family members and jobs

1 Write the characters with the radicals 宀 and 阝(right).

jiā *family, home*

家

ān *safe and stable*

安

zì *character*

字

dōu *both, all*

都

nà *that*

那

2 Write the words following the correct stroke order.

bà *father*

爸

mā *mother*

妈

jiě *elder sister*

姐

mèi *younger sister*

妹

gē *elder brother*

哥

dì *younger brother*

弟

gōngzuò *work, job*

工

作

yīshēng *doctor*

医

生

lǎoshī *teacher*

老

师

xuésheng *student*

学

生

SELF-ASSESSMENT

Complete the checklist, using the criteria below.

1 = I need a lot of help to do this.
2 = I can do this with a little help.
3 = I can do this fairly well.
4 = I can do this really well.
5 = I can do this almost perfectly.

LANGUAGE SKILL	PROGRESS	YOUR SCORE
PRONUNCIATION	• I can identify and say words with the finals "a", "e" and "i".	
VOCABULARY	• I can name at least four jobs. • I know common words and phrases used to introduce my family and other people.	
GRAMMAR	• I can make sentences with the correct word order. • I can use the adverb 也 to express "also". • I can use the adverb 都 to express "both" or "all". • I can make sentences with pronouns as modifiers and 的. • I can make noun phrases with the correct word order.	
LISTENING	• I can identify people's occupations. • I can understand people introducing their family members.	
READING	• I know the meanings of the radicals 宀 and 阝(right). • I can recognise characters used to describe a photo of someone's family and their occupations.	
SPEAKING	• I can introduce my occupation and other people's occupations. • I can introduce my family members and other people. • I can ask someone about their job and family.	
WRITING	• I can write five characters with the radicals 宀 and 阝(right), and ten common words for family members and jobs. • I can write a short passage introducing someone and their family members' occupations. • I can fill in a simple student registration form for a course.	

UNIT 4 Tā zhēn gāo 他真高！

He's really tall!

LESSON 1

Objectives

1 **Vocabulary:** words used to describe people
2 **Vocabulary:** adjectives used to describe appearance
3 **Conversation and listening:** talk about favourite people and their appearance
4 **Pronunciation:** the finals: ao, ui, en

Vocabulary

1 Write eight words to describe people using the characters in the box.

nián 年	piào 漂	zhī 知	ài 爱
míng 名	dào 道	huan 欢	xìng 姓
xǐ 喜	qīng 轻	míng 明	dà 大
xīng 星	kě 可	duō 多	liang 亮

1 ______ 5 ______

2 ______ 6 ______

3 ______ 7 ______

4 ______ 8 ______

2 Use as many adjectives as possible to describe the people in the pictures.

a ǎi 矮	d niánqīng 年轻	g lǎo 老
b gāo 高	e kě' ài 可爱	h shuài 帅
c kù 酷	f piàoliang 漂亮	

a

1 ______

b

2 ______

Conversation and listening

16

3 **Listen to the conversation and check the true statements.**

永民：他是谁？

安娜：他是刘丽的哥哥。

永民：他叫什么名字？

安娜：他叫刘明。

永民：他多大？

安娜：二十八岁。

永民：他做什么工作？

安娜：他是记者。

永民：真酷！

- ☐ 1 他是刘丽的哥哥。
- ☐ 2 刘丽的哥哥叫刘明。
- ☐ 3 刘丽二十八岁。
- ☐ 4 刘丽的哥哥是老师。
- ☐ 5 他不在学校工作。

Pronunciation

4 **Write pinyin for the words.**

1 老 ____________

2 早上 ____________

3 对不起 ____________

4 最高 ____________

5 真 ____________

6 很好 ____________

7 熊猫 ____________

8 他们 ____________

9 姚明 ____________

10 澳大利亚人 ____________

Now make sentences using the words given.

11 老师　早上

____

12 姚明　国籍

____

13 熊猫　真

____

14 我　最喜欢

____

LESSON | 2

Objectives

1 **Reading:** find basic information about someone in their personal profile
2 **Writing:** create a personal profile for yourself
3 **Grammar:** interrogative pronoun 谁 and ask about age using 多大
4 **Grammar:** numbers in Chinese
5 **Grammar:** 真/很 + adjective

Reading

17

1 Read Anna's profile and check the true statements.

☐ 1 安娜十九岁。
☐ 2 她的出生地不是伦敦。
☐ 3 安娜不喜欢篮球。
☐ 4 王玉是安娜的同学。

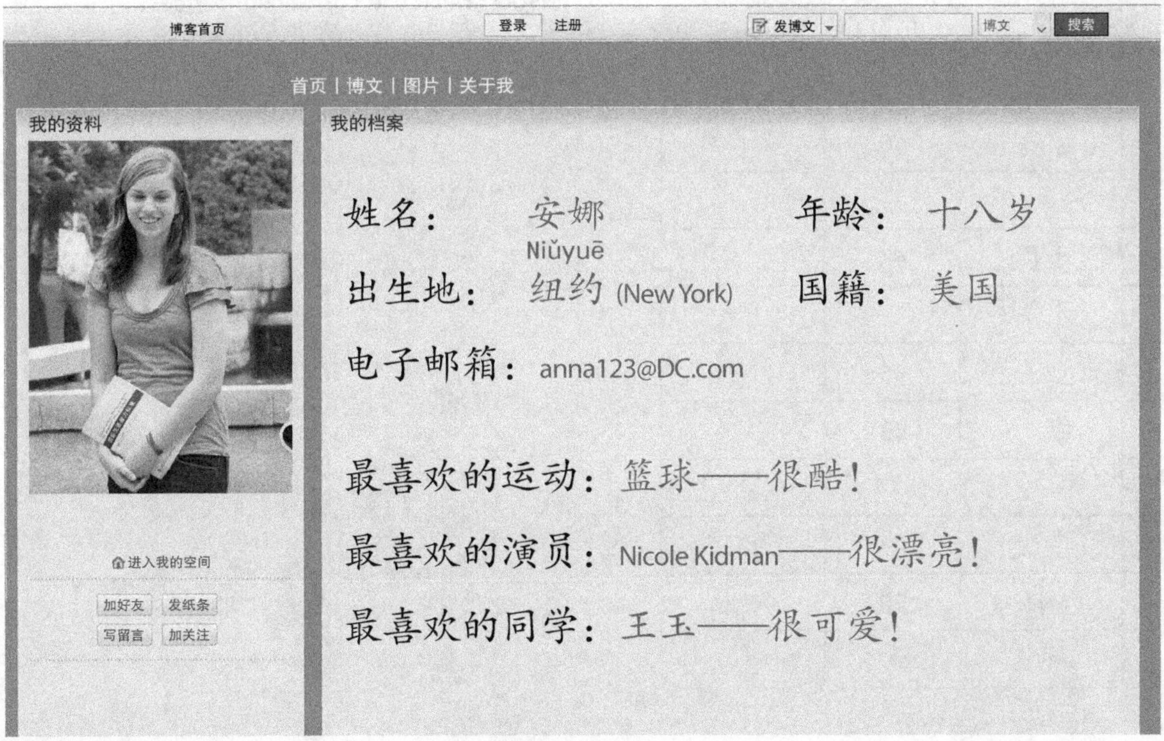

Writing

2 Answer the questions.

1 你多大？

____

2 你是哪国人？

____

3 你最喜欢的同学是谁？

____

4 你最喜欢的演员是谁？

____

Now design a profile for yourself.

____

____

____

____

Grammar

3 Write questions for the answers using 谁 or 多大.

1 Wǒ shíbā suì
我 十八 岁。

____

2 Tā shì Liú Dàwěi
他 是 刘 大伟。

____

3 Wǒ jiějie sānshí suì
我 姐姐 三十 岁。

____

4 Wǒ de tóngxué shíjiǔ suì
我 的 同学 十九 岁。

____

5 Tā hé Wáng xiānsheng zài dàxué gōngzuò
他 和 王 先生 在 大学 工作。

____

4 Complete the table with the numbers in Chinese.

Numbers	Chinese	Numbers	Chinese
11	十一	24	二十四
12	十二	38	三十八
13		45	
14	十四	47	
15	十五	52	
16		56	
17	十七	63	
18		67	六十七
19	十九	71	
21	二十一	90	九十
22		99	

18 **Now listen and order the numbers in the sequence you hear them.**

☐ **a** 19 ☐ **e** 24
☐ **b** 34 ☐ **f** 95
☐ **c** 18 ☐ **g** 80
☐ **d** 71 ☐ **h** 27

5 Put 真 or 很 in the correct places in the sentences.

1 Nǐ māma niánqīng
你 妈妈 年轻！

2 Tā kù
他 酷!

3 Wáng lǎoshī shuài
王 老师 帅!

4 Mǎkè xǐhuan Běijīng
马克 喜欢 北京。

5 Xióngmāo kě'ài
熊猫 可爱。

6 Tā gāo
她 高！

Now check the correct sentences.

☐ 7 Shǐ yīshēng hěn niánqīng
史 医生 很 年轻。

☐ 8 Tā xǐhuan hěn lánqiú
他 喜欢 很 篮球。

☐ 9 Zuò jìzhě zhēn kù
做 记者 真 酷!

☐ 10 Tā gēge zhēn gāo
他 哥哥 真 高!

☐ 11 Tā jiějie shì hěn hǎo
她 姐姐 是 很 好。

☐ 12 Yáo Míng bù zhēn shuài
姚 明 不 真 帅。

LESSON 3

Objectives

1 **Conversation:** talk about favourite people

2 **Character reading:** recognise characters with the radicals 土 and 氵

3 **Character writing:** describe where people live

4 **Vocabulary extension:** expressions used to describe people

Conversation

1 Complete the conversation with the words in the box.

yùndòngyuán 运动员	lánqiú 篮球	hěn 很
xiànzài 现在	kù 酷	ma 吗

A: 你喜欢 (1) __________ 吗?

B: 我 (2) __________ 喜欢篮球。

A: 你喜欢的篮球 (3) __________ 是谁?

B: 我最喜欢姚明。他很 (4) ________。

A: 他住在美国 (5) __________?

B: 不, 他 (6) __________ 住在上海。

Character reading

2 Match the radicals with the meanings.

1 土 — a earth

2 氵 — b water

Now match the words with the meanings.

3 演员 — c Australia

4 澳大利亚 — d Hollywood

5 现在 — e actor, actress

6 好莱坞 — f now

Character writing

3 Make sentences using the words given.

1 住在 澳大利亚

____

2 现在 好莱坞

____

Vocabulary extension

4 Match the sentences with the people in the pictures.

1 Tā gèzi gāo, duǎn tóufa, hěn shuài.
他个子高，短头发，很帅。 _____

2 Tā gèzi ǎi, hěn piàoliang.
她个子矮，很漂亮。 _____

3 Tā bù niánqīng, duǎn tóufa.
他不年轻，短头发。 _____

CHARACTER WRITING

Objectives

1 Practise six characters with the radicals 土 and 氵

2 Learn to write six common words for describing people's appearance

1 Write the words containing the radicals 土 and 氵.

chūshēngdì *place of birth*

出

生

地

Shànghǎi *Shanghai*

上

海

piàoliang *pretty*

漂

亮

zài *at, in*

在

Fǎguó *France*

法

国

yǎnyuán *actor, actress*

演

员

2 **Write the words following the correct stroke order.**

gāo *tall*

高

kě'ài *cute*

可

爱

shuài *handsome*

帅

kù *cool*

酷

niánqīng *young*

年

轻

ǎi *short*

矮

SELF-ASSESSMENT

Complete the checklist, using the criteria below.

1 = I need a lot of help to do this.

2 = I can do this with a little help.

3 = I can do this fairly well.

4 = I can do this very well.

5 = I can do this almost perfectly.

LANGUAGE SKILL	PROGRESS	YOUR SCORE
PRONUNCIATION	• I can identify and say words with the finals "ao", "ui" and "en".	
VOCABULARY	• I can say at least six adjectives about people's appearance. • I know common words and phrases used to describe people's appearance. • I can describe my favourite people and animals.	
GRAMMAR	• I can ask questions with the interrogative pronoun 谁. • I can say the numbers from 11 to 99 in Chinese. • I can ask about age using 多大. • I can use the adverbs 真 and 很 with adjectives to indicate a high degree.	
LISTENING	• I can understand simple descriptions of people's appearance.	
READING	• I know the meanings of the radicals 土 and 氵. • I can read basic information about people in their personal profiles.	
SPEAKING	• I can talk about people's appearance. • I can ask who someone is and how old they are.	
WRITING	• I can write six characters with the radicals 土 and 氵, and six common words for describing people's appearance. • I can create a simple personal profile.	

UNIT 5 Zhè shì wǒ de diànhuà hàomǎ 这是我的电话号码。

This is my phone number.

LESSON | 1

Objectives

1 **Vocabulary:** addresses and contact numbers

2 **Vocabulary:** words used to talk about addresses and contact numbers

3 **Conversation and listening:** identify contact numbers, postal and email addresses

4 **Pronunciation:** the tones of 不

Vocabulary

19

1 Listen and check the phrases or sentences you hear.

1 ☐ **a** 北京路10号

☐ **b** 大学路10号

2 ☐ **a** 邮箱地址

☐ **b** 电子邮箱

3 ☐ **a** 你的电话号码

☐ **b** 你的手机号码

4 ☐ **a** 我的电话号码是55546998。

☐ **b** 我的电话号码是46998555。

2 Write pinyin for the words.

1 电话 ____________________

2 手机 ____________________

3 号码 ____________________

4 多少 ____________________

5 地址 ____________________

6 什么 ____________________

7 路 ____________________

8 哪里 ____________________

Now write sentences using the words given.

9 电话 多少

____

10 地址 什么

____

11 你 哪里

____

12 我 电子邮箱

____

Conversation and listening

3 Complete the conversation with the sentences in the box.

David: 你的电话号码是 30541296 吗?

Angela: ______________________

David: 你的手机号码是多少?

Angela: ______________________

David: 你住在哪里?

Angela: ______________________

David: 你的电子邮箱是什么?

Angela: ______________________

1 我住在大学路 23 号。

2 我的手机号码是 16628958763。

3 是，这是我家的电话号码。

4 angela@DC.com

20 **Now listen and check your answers.**

Pronunciation

21 **4 Listen and write the correct tones for 不.**

Wǒ bu xǐhuan lánqiú
1 我 不 喜欢 篮球。

Zhè bu shì wǒ de shǒujī hàomǎ
2 这 不 是 我 的 手机 号码。

Tāmen bu gāoxìng
3 他们 不 高兴。

Ānnà bu zài yīyuàn gōngzuò
4 安娜 不 在 医院 工作。

Xióngmāo bu kě' ài
5 熊猫 不 可爱。

Ānnà bu xìng Ān
6 安娜 不 姓 安。

Now write pinyin for the words.

7 不帅 ______________

8 不酷 ______________

9 不叫 ______________

10 不认识 ______________

11 不老 ______________

12 不年轻 ______________

13 不好 ______________

14 不知道 ______________

15 不漂亮 ______________

16 不工作 ______________

LESSON 2

Objectives

1 **Vocabulary:** text message terms

2 **Reading:** understand a simple text message about contact information

3 **Writing:** give your contact details

4 **Grammar:** question word 多少

5 **Grammar:** word order of Chinese addresses

6 **Pronunciation:** the pronunciation of the number "1"

Vocabulary

1 Match the words with the meanings.

1 收件箱 (shōujiànxiāng)	a send
2 收到 (shōudào)	b new message
3 发送 (fāsòng)	c exit, go back
4 退出 (tuìchū)	d receive
5 新 短信 (xīn duǎnxìn)	e inbox

Reading

22

2 Read the text message and answer the questions.

1 王玉知道永民住在哪里吗？

____

2 永民可以给王玉打电话吗？

____

3 王玉的电话号码是多少？

____

Writing

3 Write a message to your friend telling him/her your address and home phone number.

____

____

____

Grammar

4 Write questions for the answers using 多少.

Wǒ de fángjiān hào shì
1 我 的 房间 号 是 3608。

____

Tā de diànhuà hàomǎ shì
2 他 的 电话 号码 是 86752345。

____

Wáng Yù zhù zài Dàxué Lù hào
3 王 玉 住 在 大学 路 24 号。

____

Shǐdìfū de shǒujī hàomǎ shì
4 史蒂夫 的 手机 号码 是 12081345761。

____

Now answer the questions with your own information.

Nǐ de diànhuà hàomǎ shì duōshao
5 你的 电话 号码 是 多少？

____

Nǐ zhù zài nǎli
6 你 住 在 哪里？

____

Nǐ de fángjiān hào shì duōshao
7 你的 房间 号 是 多少？

____

5 Put the words in the correct order to make addresses.

hào fángjiān hào Dàxué Lù
1 1319号 房间 / 23 号 / 大学 路 /
Dàxuéshēng gōngyù
大学生 公寓

____

Gōngyuán Lù Běijīng hào Zhōngguó
2 公园 路 / 北京 / 26 号 / 中国

____

hào Shànghǎi gōngyù Shànghǎi Lù
3 75 号 / 上海 公寓 / 上海 路

____

hào Běijīng Lù
4 38 号 / 北京 路

____

Dàxué Lù Lúndūn gōngyù hào
5 大学 路 / 伦敦 公寓 / 15 号

____

Dàxuéshēng gōngyù hào fángjiān
6 大学生 公寓 / 709 号 房间

____

6 Write pinyin for the numbers.

1 我的电话号码是 8311650179。

____

2 我住在北京路 1 号。

____

3 大学生公寓 119 号房间

____

4 我哥哥 31 岁。

____

5 王玉的新家在公园路 12 号。

____

6 一二三四五

____

7 她的手机号码是 10922103318。

____

8 他住在 21 号房间。

____

9 今天是三月二号，星期一。

____

10 11 个房间

____

LESSON | 3

Objectives

1 **Writing:** ask for addresses and contact numbers

2 **Character reading:** recognise characters with the radicals 讠 and 辶

3 **Character writing:** write about contact numbers

4 **Vocabulary extension:** words and word order of addresses

Writing

1 Write a text message to your friend asking for his/her home address, email address and home phone number.

____

____

____

Character reading

2 Match the radicals with the meanings.

1 讠	a walk
2 辶	b speech

Now match the words with the meanings.

3 认识	c this
4 谁	d exit
5 这	e who
6 退出	f know

Character writing

3 Make sentences using the words given.

1 知道　　号码

____

2 这　　电话

____

Vocabulary extension

4 Write the addresses on the envelopes in Chinese.

1 王娜, Room 103, Student Apartment No. 28 Garden Street, Beijing, China

2 刘玉, No. 1 Beijing Street, Xinrong (新荣) District, Xianghua (向华) City, Sichuan Province, China

CHARACTER WRITING

Objectives

1 Practise five characters with the radicals 讠 and 辶

2 Learn to write seven common words for addresses and contact numbers

1 Write the words containing the radicals 讠 and 辶.

jìzhě *journalist*

记

者

shéi *who*

谁

zhè *this*

这

fāsòng *send*

发

送

tuìchū *exit*

退

出

2 Write the words following the correct stroke order.

diànhuà *telephone*

电

话

hàomǎ *number*

号

码

duōshao *what, how many/much*

多

少

dìzhǐ *address*

地

址

lù *road*

路

gōngyù *flat*

公

寓

fángjiān *room*

房

间

SELF-ASSESSMENT

Complete the checklist, using the criteria below.

1 = I need a lot of help to do this.
2 = I can do this with a little help.
3 = I can do this fairly well.
4 = I can do this very well.
5 = I can do this almost perfectly.

LANGUAGE SKILL	PROGRESS	YOUR SCORE
PRONUNCIATION	• I can identify and say the word 不 in different phrases with the correct tones. • I can pronounce the number "1" in different expressions correctly.	
VOCABULARY	• I can express addresses and contact numbers. • I know common text message terms.	
GRAMMAR	• I can ask questions about contact numbers and addresses using 多少. • I know the correct word order of Chinese addresses.	
LISTENING	• I can identify contact numbers, postal addresses and email addresses.	
READING	• I know the meanings of the radicals 讠 and 辶. • I can recognise characters to understand simple text messages about addresses and contact numbers.	
SPEAKING	• I can ask for contact numbers and addresses. • I can say contact numbers and addresses.	
WRITING	• I can write five characters with the radicals 讠 and 辶, and seven common words for addresses and contact numbers. • I can write simple messages about contact numbers.	

UNIT 6 Jīntiān jǐ hào 今天 几 号?

What's the date today?

LESSON 1

Objectives

1 **Vocabulary:** months

2 **Vocabulary:** days of the week

3 **Vocabulary:** days of the week, months and dates

4 **Conversation and listening:** talk about birthdays and make invitations

5 **Pronunciation:** the initials: j, q, x

Vocabulary

1 Match the Chinese months with the English ones.

1 二月	a January
2 五月	b February
3 一月	c March
4 七月	d May
5 九月	e June
6 十二月	f July
7 三月	g August
8 六月	h September
9 十月	i October
10 八月	j December

2 Put the days of the week in the correct order.

a Xīngqīwǔ 星期五

b Xīngqīsān 星期三

c Xīngqīyī 星期一

d Xīngqītiān 星期天

e Xīngqī' èr 星期二

f Xīngqīliù 星期六

g Xīngqīsì 星期四

The correct order is ______________________.

3 Match the questions with the answers.

1 Jīntiān jǐ hào 今天 几 号? ______

2 Jīntiān xīngqī jǐ 今天 星期 几? ______

3 Xīngqīliù shì jǐ hào 星期六 是 几 号? ______

4 Jiǔyuè yī hào shì Xīngqīwǔ ma 九月 一 号 是 星期五 吗? ______

5 Xīngqītiān shì èrshíqī hào ma 星期天 是 二十七 号 吗? ______

a Jīntiān Xīngqī' èr 今天 星期二。

b Shì Jiǔyuè yī hào shì Xīngqīwǔ 是，九月 一 号 是 星期五。

c Jīntiān Sānyuè èr hào 今天 三月 二 号。

d Xīngqīliù shì Qīyuè wǔ hào 星期六 是 七月 五 号。

e Bú shì Xīngqītiān shì èrshíliù hào 不是，星期天 是 二十六 号。

Conversation and listening

4 Put the sentences in the correct order to make a conversation.

a 你的生日是几月几号?

b 我十八岁。

c 我的生日是十月四号。

d 我请你去"北京厨房"吃饭，怎么样?

e 谢谢。

f 王娜，你多大?

g 太好了，谢谢！那里的中餐很好吃。

h 是今天吗? 生日快乐!

The correct order is ______________________.

23 **Now listen to the conversation and check the true statements.**

☐ 1 王娜的生日是十月四号。

☐ 2 今天不是十月四号。

☐ 3 王娜二十岁。

☐ 4 她喜欢去"北京厨房"。

Pronunciation

5 Write pinyin for the words.

1 星期几 ______________

2 家 ______________

3 年轻 ______________

4 叫 ______________

5 今天 ______________

6 北京 ______________

7 见 ______________

8 房间 ______________

9 请 ______________

10 去 ______________

11 九十七 ______________

12 小姐 ______________

13 谢谢 ______________

14 新 ______________

15 姓 ______________

16 学生 ______________

LESSON 2

Objectives

1 **Vocabulary:** everyday activities
2 **Reading:** understand activities in a weekly planner
3 **Writing:** create a weekly planner
4 **Grammar:** months and dates
5 **Grammar:** sentences without verbs
6 **Grammar:** make invitations using 请

Vocabulary

1 Match the words with the meanings.

1 pàiduì 派对	a meet up
2 jiànmiàn 见面	b read a book
3 chīfàn 吃饭	c learn Chinese
4 kàn shū 看 书	d have a meal
5 qù yīyuàn 去 医院	e play basketball
6 xué Zhōngwén 学 中文	f party
7 shàngbān 上班	g go to hospital
8 dǎ lánqiú 打 篮球	h go to work

Reading

24

2 Read Yeong-min's weekly planner and answer the questions.

1 永民几号去医院?

____

2 永民星期几学中文?

____

3 妈妈的生日派对是几月几号?

____

三月七日 — 九日

	9:00—12:00	12:00—15:00	15:00—18:00	18:00—21:00
星期一	学中文	跟史蒂夫见面	上班	请王玉吃饭
星期二		上班	打篮球	妈妈的生日派对
星期三	学中文		去医院	跟马克去吃中餐

Writing

3 Write your own weekly planner.

	9:00—12:00	12:00—15:00	15:00—18:00	18:00—21:00
星期一				
星期二				
星期三				

Grammar

4 Put the dates in order from the earliest to the latest.

a 三月十号

b 八月二十号

c 八月四号

d 六月十九号

e 三月二十八号

f 四月三十号

The correct order is ______________________.

Now write six sentences about your activities over the next three days.

1 ______________________

2 ______________________

3 ______________________

4 ______________________

5 ______________________

6 ______________________

5 Check the correct sentences.

☐ 1 Tā mèimei hěn kě' ài
她 妹妹 很 可爱！

☐ 2 Jīntiān shì shíliù hào
今天 是 十六 号。

☐ 3 Wáng yīshēng shì sānshí suì
王 医生 是 三十 岁。

☐ 4 Jīntiān Xīngqīyī
今天 星期一。

☐ 5 Wǒ bù gāoxìng
我 不 高兴。

Now write the sentences in Chinese.

6 Today is Friday.

____

7 His mother is 40 years old.

____

8 Yao Ming is really cool!

____

9 Her brother is very tall.

____

10 What date is today?

____

6 Make sentences using 请 and the words given.

1 Wáng Yù 王 玉 | qù pàiduì 去 派对 | wǒ 我

____

2 Mǎkè 马克 | lǎoshī 老师 | chīfàn 吃饭

____

3 Ānnà 安娜 | qù tā jiā 去 她 家 | Yǒngmín 永民

____

4 Shǐdìfū 史蒂夫 | chī zhōngcān 吃 中餐 | Wáng Yù 王 玉

____

Now write two sentences involving yourself using 请.

5 ______________________

6 ______________________

LESSON 3

Objectives

1 **Vocabulary:** public holidays in China

2 **Character reading:** recognise characters with the radicals 月 and 扌

3 **Character writing:** write about everyday activities

4 **Vocabulary extension:** days and dates

Vocabulary

1 **Complete the table with the Chinese public holidays in 2022 in the box.**

a	Yuándàn 元旦	New Year	一月一日
b	Qīngmíngjié 清明节	Tomb Sweeping Festival	四月五日
c	Láodòngjié 劳动节	May Day	五月一日
d	Duānwǔjié 端午节	Dragon Boat Festival	六月三日
e	Zhōngqiūjié 中秋节	Mid-Autumn Festival	九月十一日
f	Guóqìngjié 国庆节	National Day	十月一日

月份	节日	月份	节日
January		July	
February		August	
March		September	
April		October	
May		November	
June		December	

Character reading

2 **Match the radicals with the meanings.**

1 月   a hand

2 扌   b moon

Now match the words with the meanings.

3 二月   c Friday

4 星期五   d nurse

5 打篮球   e February

6 护士   f play basketball

Character writing

3 **Make sentences using the words given.**

1 星期五   打篮球

____

2 给   打电话

____

Vocabulary extension

4 **Complete the table with the appropriate days and dates.**

Previous	Present	Next
qùnián 去年		
	zhège yuè 这个 月	
		xiàge xīngqī 下个 星期
	jīntiān 今天	
Shíyuè 十月		

CHARACTER WRITING

Objectives

1 Practise four characters with the radicals 月 and 扌

2 Learn to write nine common words for dates and daily activities

1 Write the words containing the radicals 月 and 扌.

yuè *month*

月 月 月 月

月

xīngqī *week*

星 星 星 星 星 星 星 星 星

星

期 期 期 期 期 期 期 期 期 期 期 期

期

dǎ *play*

打 打 打 打 打

打

hùshi *nurse*

护 护 护 护 护 护 护

护

士 士 士

士

2 Write the words following the correct stroke order.

jīntiān *today*

今 今 今 今

今

天 天 天 天

天

jǐhào *what date*

几 几

几

号 号 号 号 号

号

chīfàn *have a meal*

吃	吃	吃	吃	吃	吃

吃

饭	饭	饭	饭	饭	饭
饭					

饭

jiànmiàn *meet up*

见	见	见	见		

见

面	面	面	面	面	面
面	面	面			

面

qù *go*

去	去	去	去	去	

去

kànshū *read a book*

看	看	看	看	看	看
看	看	看			

看

书	书	书	书		

书

xué *learn*

学	学	学	学	学	学
学	学				

学

shàngbān *go to work*

上	上	上			

上

班	班	班	班	班	班
班	班	班	班		

班

zuò *do*

做	做	做	做	做	做
做	做	做	做	做	

做

SELF-ASSESSMENT

Complete the checklist, using the criteria below.

1 = I need a lot of help to do this.
2 = I can do this with a little help.
3 = I can do this fairly well.
4 = I can do this very well.
5 = I can do this almost perfectly.

LANGUAGE SKILL	PROGRESS	YOUR SCORE
PRONUNCIATION	• I can identify and say words with the initials "j", "q" and "x".	
VOCABULARY	• I know the words for months and days of the week. • I know how to express dates. • I know common words and phrases used to make invitations. • I know five words for everyday activities. • I can name five public holidays in China.	
GRAMMAR	• I can express dates and months. • I can make sentences without verbs to express age, dates, days of the week and time. • I can make invitations using 请.	
LISTENING	• I can identify days of the week, months and dates. • I can understand people talking about what day or date something will happen. • I can understand people's birth dates. • I can understand people making invitations.	
READING	• I know the meanings of the radicals 月 and 扌. • I can understand activities in a weekly planner.	
SPEAKING	• I can ask for and say dates and days. • I can say my date of birth. • I can make simple invitations.	
WRITING	• I can write four characters with the radicals 月 and 扌, and nine common words for dates and daily activities. • I can complete a weekly planner.	

UNIT 7 八点见！ (Bā diǎn jiàn)

See you at eight!

LESSON 1

Objectives

1 **Vocabulary:** time

2 **Vocabulary:** words used to talk about social plans

3 **Conversation and listening:** plan a social activity

4 **Pronunciation:** difference between "u" and "ü"

5 **Grammar:** express future tense using the verb 要

Vocabulary

25

1 Number the times in the order you hear them.

☐ a 5:20	☐ e 2:15
☐ b 1:25	☐ f 6:30
☐ c 10:40	☐ g 11:55
☐ d 3:00	☐ h 12:45

2 Match the words with the meanings.

1 shíjiān 时间	a weekend
2 zhōumò 周末	b time
3 kāishǐ 开始	c tomorrow
4 jìhuà 计划	d start
5 míngtiān 明天	e plan

Conversation and listening

3 Complete the conversation with the words and phrases in the box.

wǎnshang 晚上	ménkǒu 门口	tài hǎo le 太好了
jǐ diǎn 几点	yǒu shíjiān 有时间	kàn diànyǐng 看电影

永民：星期一去 (1) ________，好吗？

安娜：星期一是几号？

永民：星期一是二十号。

安娜：好，我 (2) ________。我们看什么电影？

永民：你喜欢美国电影吗？

安娜：我很喜欢。

永民：(3) ________。我们看 New York 1982，怎么样？

安娜：好。(4) ________？

永民：(5) ________ 九点半，可以吗？

安娜：没问题。星期一九点在电影院 (6) ________ 见。

26 Now listen to the conversation and check the true statements.

☐ 7 星期一是二十二号。

☐ 8 永民和安娜星期一看电影。

☐ 9 安娜喜欢美国电影。

☐ 10 电影的名字叫New York 1983。

☐ 11 电影九点三十分开始。

Pronunciation

4 Check the correct pinyin for the words.

1 退出	☐ a tuìchū	☐ b tuìqū
2 看书	☐ a kàn xū	☐ b kàn shū
3 动物	☐ a dòngwù	☐ b dòngyù
4 护士	☐ a hùshi	☐ b qùshi
5 公寓	☐ a gōngxù	☐ b gōngyù
6 很酷	☐ a hěn kù	☐ b hěn gù
7 厨房	☐ a chúfáng	☐ b qúfáng
8 不好	☐ a xù hǎo	☐ b bù hǎo
9 马路	☐ a mǎlù	☐ b mǎlù
10 五天	☐ a wǔ tiān	☐ b yǔ tiān

27 Now listen and check your answers.

Grammar

5 Put 要 in the correct places in the sentences.

Tā qù Lúndūn
1 他 去 伦敦。

Tāmen wǎnshang xué Yīngyǔ
2 他们 晚上 学 英语。

Zhōumò wǒ kàn yéye nǎinai
3 周末 我 看 爷爷 奶奶。

Wǒ xiàwǔ gēn péngyou dǎ lánqiú
4 我 下午 跟 朋友 打 篮球。

Míngtiān wǒ gěi tā xiě diànzǐ yóujiàn
5 明天 我 给 她 写 电子 邮件。

Now complete the conversations using 要 and the words in brackets.

Nǐ Xīngqīliù zuò shénme
6 A: 你 星期六 做 什么?

B: ________________________________。

xué Zhōngwén
(学 中文)

Nǐ xiàwǔ qù nǎli
7 A: 你 下午 去 哪里?

B: ________________________________。

yīyuàn
(医院)

Nǐ wǎnshang gēn shéi chī zhōngcān
8 A: 你 晚上 跟 谁 吃 中餐?

B: ________________________________。

mèimei
(妹妹)

Nǐ zhège zhōumò yǒu shénme jìhuà
9 A: 你 这个 周末 有 什么 计划?

B: ________________________________。

tīng yīnyuèhuì
(听 音乐会)

LESSON 2

Objectives

1 **Vocabulary:** time, family members and everyday activities
2 **Grammar:** adverbial expressions of time
3 **Grammar:** different ways of telling the time
4 **Reading:** understand activities in a weekend planner
5 **Writing:** create a weekend planner

Vocabulary

1 Circle the odd word out in each line.

1 a pǎobù 跑步 b tīng yīnyuè 听 音乐 c dǎ lánqiú 打 篮球
2 a jìzhě 记者 b yéye 爷爷 c nǎinai 奶奶
3 a bókè 博客 b diànyǐng 电影 c diànzǐ yóujiàn 电子 邮件
4 a shàngwǔ 上午 b wǎnshang 晚上 c míngtiān 明天
5 a dào 到 b yìqǐ 一起 c jiàn 见
6 a chànggē 唱歌 b Zhōngwén 中文 c Yīngyǔ 英语
7 a wǎnfàn 晚饭 b zhōngcān 中餐 c Rìběncài 日本菜
8 a xiě 写 b tīng 听 c kù 酷

Now make sentences using the words given.

9 上午　打篮球

____

10 一起　吃日本菜

____

Grammar

2 Circle the time expressions in the sentences.

1 Wǒ Xīngqī' èr wǎnshang kàn diànyǐng
我 星期二 晚上 看 电影。

2 Nǐmen míngtiān zuò shénme
你们 明天 做 什么？

3 Xiàwǔ sì diǎn nǐ yào kàn yīshēng
下午 四 点 你 要 看 医生。

Now write the sentences in Chinese.

4 We'll meet at the entrance of the university at 10:30 tomorrow morning.

____

5 I exercise on Wednesday afternoon.

____

6 I will go to the concert with friends on Sunday.

____

3 Tell each of these times in two ways and write them down.

Time	Expression 1	Expression 2
7:30		
10:15		
9:45		
12:30		
6:15		
2:45		

Reading

28

4 Read Anna's weekend planner and check the true statements.

☐ 1 安娜星期六上午不在家。

☐ 2 她星期六到"妈妈厨房"吃饭。

☐ 3 她星期六下午打篮球。

☐ 4 她星期六晚上跟马克听音乐会。

☐ 5 马克的生日是星期六。

☐ 6 安娜星期日中午在家。

☐ 7 电影两点一刻开始。

☐ 8 安娜星期日晚上请马克吃日本菜。

周末计划簿		星期六
要做的事	上午	在家写博客
	中午	12:45 在"妈妈厨房"吃中餐
	下午	3:30 打篮球
	晚上	8:00 跟王玉听音乐会
备忘录		给马克写生日卡
		星期日
要做的事	上午	7:00 跟史蒂夫跑步
	中午	12:00 在家吃饭
	下午	2:15 跟朋友看电影
	晚上	6:30 马克的生日，请他吃韩国菜
备忘录		给老师写电子邮件

Writing

5 Write a weekend planner for yourself.

周末计划簿		星期六
要做的事	上午	
	中午	
	下午	
	晚上	
备忘录		
		星期日
要做的事	上午	
	中午	
	下午	
	晚上	
备忘录		

Now write six sentences about your activities in the weekend planner using 要.

1 ____________________

2 ____________________

3 ____________________

4 ____________________

5 ____________________

6 ____________________

LESSON 3

Objectives

1 **Reading:** understand people's weekly plan

2 **Character reading:** recognise characters with the radicals 门 and 𧾷

3 **Character writing:** plan social activities

4 **Vocabulary extension:** leisure activities

Reading

29

1 Read Steve's online messages with his friends and complete the invitation message at the end.

Steve

你们星期几有时间？我们一起吃饭，好吗？

Anna

我星期二晚上打篮球，星期三学唱歌。

Yeong-min

我星期一学中文，星期六听音乐会。我星期三、星期五有时间。

Wang Yu

星期四是妈妈的生日，我要在家吃饭。星期天跟朋友看电影。

Steve

星期 ______ 大家都有时间，我们一起吃晚饭吧。

Character reading

2 Match the radicals with the meanings.

1 门	a foot
2 𧾷	b gate

Now match the words with the meanings.

3 路	c entrance, doorway
4 时间	d jog
5 跑步	e time
6 门口	f road

Character writing

3 Make sentences using the words given.

1 时间　跑步

____

2 门口　见

____

Vocabulary extension

4 Write four sentences using the words in the box.

yóuyǒng 游泳	mǎi dōngxi 买 东西
kàn diànshì 看 电视	kàn bǐsài 看 比赛

1 ______________________________

2 ______________________________

3 ______________________________

4 ______________________________

CHARACTER WRITING

Objectives

1 Practise four characters with the radicals 门 and 𧾷

2 Learn to write nine common words for time expressions and daily activities

1 Write the words containing the radicals 门 and 𧾷.

pǎobù *jog*

跑

步

shíjiān *time*

时

间

mén *door*

门

gēn *with*

跟

2 Write the characters following the correct stroke order.

fēn *minute*

分

kè *quarter*

刻

bàn *half*

半

diǎn *o'clock*

点

wǎn *evening*

晚

zhōngwǔ *noon*

中

午

yīnyuè *music*

音

乐

diànyǐng *film, movie*

电

影

chànggē *sing a song*

唱

歌

SELF-ASSESSMENT

Complete the checklist, using the criteria below.

1 = I need a lot of help to do this.

2 = I can do this with a little help.

3 = I can do this fairly well.

4 = I can do this very well.

5 = I can do this almost perfectly.

LANGUAGE SKILL	PROGRESS	YOUR SCORE
PRONUNCIATION	• I can identify and say words with the finals "u" and "ü".	
VOCABULARY	• I know the words and expressions used to say the time. • I know common words and expressions used to plan a social activity.	
GRAMMAR	• I can make sentences with adverbial expressions of time. • I can express the time in two different ways. • I can express future actions using the verb 要.	
LISTENING	• I can identify the time. • I can understand people planning simple social activities.	
READING	• I know the meanings of the radicals 门 and 𧾷. • I can understand characters used to tell the time. • I can understand activities in a weekend planner.	
SPEAKING	• I can ask for and tell the time. • I can make simple plans for social activities.	
WRITING	• I can write four characters with the radicals 门 and 𧾷, and nine common words for time expressions and daily activities. • I can create a weekend planner.	

UNIT 8 Duōshao qián 多少 钱？

How much is it?

LESSON 1

Objectives

1 **Vocabulary:** prices
2 **Vocabulary:** colours and clothes
3 **Vocabulary:** colours of things
4 **Conversation and listening:** buy clothes
5 **Conversation:** haggle over the price
6 **Pronunciation:** the tones of 一

Vocabulary

1 Write the prices in Chinese characters.

1 ¥154 ____________________

2 ¥91 ____________________

3 ¥898 ____________________

30

2 Number the clothes items in the order you hear them.

☐ a hóngsè de xié 红色 的 鞋

☐ b hēisè de máoyī 黑色 的 毛衣

☐ c báisè de xù 白色 的 T恤

☐ d lǜsè de qúnzi 绿色 的 裙子

☐ e lánsè de kùzi 蓝色 的 裤子

☐ f huángsè de dàyī 黄色 的 大衣

3 Match the colours with the things.

1 hēisè 黑色

2 báisè 白色

3 lǜsè 绿色

4 huángsè 黄色

5 hóngsè 红色

a

b

c

d

e

Conversation and listening

4 Complete the conversation with the words in the box.

duìbuqǐ 对不起	dàyī 大衣	le 了	shìshi 试试
zěnmeyàng 怎么样	búcuò 不错	tiáo 条	xǐhuan 喜欢

售货员：这件 (1) ________ 怎么样？

王玉：太大 (2) ________！

售货员：这 (3) ________ 裤子呢？

王玉：我不 (4) ________ 黑色。

售货员：这件毛衣 (5) ________？

王玉：(6) ________。我可以 (7) ________ 吗？

售货员：(8) ________，不可以。

王玉：那我不买了。

31 **Now listen to the conversation and check the true statements.**

☐ 9 这件大衣太大。

☐ 10 王玉喜欢黑色。

☐ 11 这件毛衣好看。

☐ 12 王玉可以试毛衣。

☐ 13 王玉没有买毛衣。

Conversation

5 Put the sentences in the correct order to make a conversation.

a Xièxie
谢谢。

b Sānbǎi jiǔshí kuài
三百 九十 块。

c Duìbuqǐ sānbǎi kuài zhège jiàqián hěn piányi
对不起，三百 块 这个 价钱 很 便宜。

d Liǎngbǎi kuài zěnmeyàng
两百 块 怎么样？

e Zhè tiáo hóngsè de qúnzi hěn hǎokàn Duōshao qián
这 条 红色 的 裙子 很 好看！多少 钱？

f Tài guì le Piányi yīdiǎnr ba
太 贵 了。便宜 一点儿 吧。

g Hǎo ba Gěi nǐ qián
好吧。给 你 钱。

h Sānbǎi kuài ba
三百 块 吧。

The correct order is ________________.

Pronunciation

6 Write pinyin for the phrases, including the correct tone for 一 in spoken Chinese.

1 一起 ________________

2 一百块 ________________

3 一双鞋 ________________

4 一件大衣 ________________

LESSON | 2

Objectives

1 **Vocabulary:** shopping places in the city
2 **Reading:** understand descriptions of purchases
3 **Writing:** write a blog entry about things you bought
4 **Grammar:** measure words
5 **Grammar:** numerals 二 and 两
6 **Grammar:** express the completion of an action using 了

Vocabulary

1 Match the words with the meanings.

1 购物中心	a bookshop
2 服装市场	b supermarket
3 书店	c clothes market
4 超市	d shopping centre

Reading

32

2 Read Wang Yu's blog.

Beijing Life 主页 博客 相册 档案 互动

发表文章

四月十五日 星期日

我和高云是好朋友。他在书店工作了两年，我在他的书店买了很多书。

分享 | 评论 (06) | 阅读 (207) | 固定链接 | 发表于15:36

星期六我跟姐姐去了服装市场。我买了一件红色的大衣，九百块。真贵！但是很漂亮！

分享 | 评论 (06) | 阅读 (315) | 固定链接 | 发表于15:48

我很喜欢买T恤。你知道我买了多少件T 恤吗？三十件。十件白色的、八件红色的、六件蓝色的和六件黄色的。

分享 | 评论 (16) | 阅读 (476) | 固定链接 | 发表于16:29

Now check the true statements.

☐ 1 高云是王玉的好朋友。
☐ 2 高云在书店工作了四年。
☐ 3 王玉星期六在服装市场买了一件大衣。
☐ 4 大衣不便宜，但是很漂亮。
☐ 5 王玉有三十一件T恤。
☐ 6 白色的T恤最多。
☐ 7 王玉没有蓝色的T恤。
☐ 8 王玉不喜欢红色。

Writing

3 Write a blog entry about the things you bought recently. Use the blog from Activity 2 to help you.

Grammar

4 Complete the phrases with the words in the box.

tiáo 条	shuāng 双	jiàn 件	gè 个

1 yì 一 ____________ kùzi 裤子

2 yì 一 ____________ shǒu 手

3 yí 一 ____________ xù T恤

4 yì 一 ____________ máojīn 毛巾

5 yí 一 ____________ píngguǒ 苹果

6 yì 一 ____________ lù 路

7 yì 一 ____________ qúnzi 裙子

8 yì 一 ____________ yǎnjing 眼睛

9 yí 一 ____________ yuè 月

10 yí 一 ____________ péngyou 朋友

11 yí 一 ____________ dàyī 大衣

12 yì 一 ____________ xié 鞋

13 yí 一 ____________ rén 人

14 yí 一 ____________ máoyī 毛衣

15 yí 一 ____________ xīngqī 星期

5 Write the words in Chinese using 二 or 两.

1 Tuesday ____________

2 two people ____________

3 February ____________

4 twelve students ____________

5 2 December ____________

6 ¥20 ____________

7 2:10 pm ____________

8 325 ____________

6 Put 了 in the correct places in the sentences.

1 Shàng gè zhōumò wǒ kàn yéye nǎinai
上 个 周末 我 看 爷爷 奶奶。

2 Wǒ zài Měiguó rènshi hěn duō péngyou
我 在 美国 认识 很 多 朋友。

3 Tā Xīngqīsān qù Shànghǎi
她 星期三 去 上海。

4 Wǒ zài zhèli zhù sān nián
我 在 这里 住 三 年 。

5 Tā bàba zhīdào zhè jiàn shì
他 爸爸 知道 这 件 事。

Now write the sentences in Chinese.

6 They have gone to Shanghai.

____

7 I asked him where he lives.

____

8 Anna bought two pairs of shoes.

____

9 Mark arrived at the university at 8 o'clock.

____

LESSON | 3

Objectives

1 **Listening:** understand an introduction from a shop assistant

2 **Character reading:** recognise characters with the radicals 衤 and 贝

3 **Character writing:** write about shopping

4 **Vocabulary extension:** items of clothing

Listening

33

1 Listen to Ma Xiaoyu's introduction and answer the questions.

大家好！我是马小玉。我是中国人，住在北京。我在超市工作。这个超市不大，也不太有名，但是有很多英国、美国和日本的东西，价钱也不贵。周末很多人来这里买东西。请你们也来这里买东西吧。

1 她叫什么名字？

____

2 她是哪国人？住在哪里？

____

3 她在哪里工作？那里怎么样？

____

Character reading

2 Match the radicals with the meanings.

1 衤 a shell

2 贝 b clothes

Now match the words with the meanings.

3 裙子 c expensive

4 衬衫 d shopping

5 贵 e skirt

6 购物 f shirt

Character writing

3 Make sentences using the words given.

1 购物 贵

____

2 买 裙子

____

Vocabulary extension

4 Write six sentences about your clothes, including their colours. Use the following words to help you.

wéijīn 围巾	chènshān 衬衫	duǎnkù 短裤
màozi 帽子	niúzǎikù 牛仔裤	liányīqún 连衣裙

1 ______________________________

2 ______________________________

3 ______________________________

4 ______________________________

5 ______________________________

6 ______________________________

CHARACTER WRITING

Objectives

1 Practise eight characters with the radicals 衤 and 贝

2 Learn to write eight common words for clothes, colours and places

1 Write the words containing the radicals 衤 and 贝.

qún *skirt*

裙

kù *trousers*

裤

chènshān *shirt*

衬

衫

shòuhuòyuán *shop assistant*

售

货

员

guì *expensive*

贵

gòu *buy*

购

2 **Write the words following the correct stroke order.**

yīfu *clothes*

衣

服

xié *shoes*

鞋

hóng *red*

红

hēi *black*

黑

lán *blue*

蓝

bái *white*

白

chāoshì *supermarket*

超

市

diàn *shop*

店

SELF-ASSESSMENT

Complete the checklist, using the criteria below.

1 = I need a lot of help to do this.
2 = I can do this with a little help.
3 = I can do this fairly well.
4 = I can do this very well.
5 = I can do this almost perfectly.

LANGUAGE SKILL	PROGRESS	YOUR SCORE
PRONUNCIATION	• I can identify and say the tones of 一 in different phrases.	
VOCABULARY	• I can name six colours. • I can name six items of clothing. • I can express prices correctly. • I know the words for four places where people can buy things.	
GRAMMAR	• I can use the measure words 个, 条, 件 and 双 correctly. • I can use 二 when counting or expressing sequence. • I can use 两 to express quantity. • I can use the particle 了 to express the completion of an action.	
LISTENING	• I can identify clothes, colours and prices. • I can understand conversations about buying things.	
READING	• I know the meanings of the radicals 衤 and 贝. • I can understand descriptions of a product's price and colour.	
SPEAKING	• I can describe the colour and price of different clothes. • I can express likes and dislikes about clothes. • I can negotiate prices.	
WRITING	• I can write eight characters with the radicals 衤 and 贝, and eight common words for clothes, colours and places. • I can write simple blog entries about things I have bought.	

UNIT 9 Bù yuǎn 不远！

It's not far!

LESSON 1

Objectives

1. **Vocabulary:** places in the neighbourhood
2. **Vocabulary:** directions and locations
3. **Conversation and listening:** identify locations and directions of places
4. **Conversation and listening:** ask for and give directions
5. **Pronunciation:** retroflex "r"

Vocabulary

1 Match the words with the meanings.

1 fànguǎn 饭馆	a post office
2 xǐshǒujiān 洗手间	b bookshop
3 yínháng 银行	c restaurant
4 yóujú 邮局	d bank
5 shūdiàn 书店	e park
6 gōngyuán 公园	f toilet

Now complete the sentence with the words above .

Wǒ jiā fùjìn yǒu

7 我家附近有 ________________

________________________________。

2 Look at the map and complete the sentences with the words in the box.

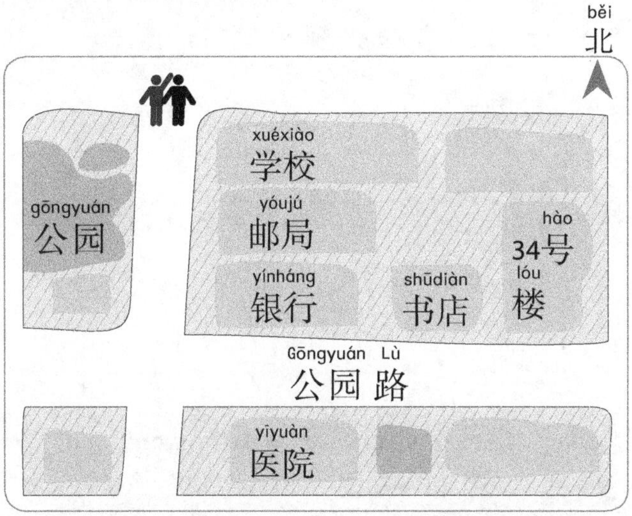

dōngbian 东边	běibian 北边
xībian 西边	nánbian 南边

Gōngyuán zài yóujú de
1 公园 在邮局的 ____________。

Xuéxiào zài yóujú de
2 学校 在邮局的 ____________。

Shūdiàn zài yínháng de
3 书店 在 银行 的 ____________。

Yīyuàn zài yínháng de
4 医院 在 银行 的 ____________。

Gōngyuán Lù zài yīyuàn de
5 公园 路在 医院 的 ____________。

hào lóu zài shūdiàn de
6 34 号 楼在 书店 的 ____________。

Conversation and listening

34

3 **Listen to the conversation and complete the sentences.**

A: 请问，中国银行在哪儿？
B: 在医院前边。
A: 离这儿远不远？
B: 不远。
A: 怎么走？
B: 往东边走八分钟左右。
A: 谢谢。

1 他要去 ______________。

2 银行在医院 __________。

3 他要往 __________ 走 ________ 分钟。

4 **Complete the conversation with the words in the box.**

zài 在	yóujú 邮局	yǒu méiyǒu 有 没有
hòubian 后边	nǎbiān 哪边	wǔ fēn zhōng 五 分 钟

A: 请问，附近 (1) ________ 银行？
B: 有，(2) _________ 上海路。
A: 往 (3) __________ 走？
B: 往西边走 (4) __________ ，在邮局 (5) _________ 。
A: 是公园前边的 (6) _________ 吗？
B: 是的。

35

Now listen to the conversation and check the true statements.

☐ 7 附近没有银行。
☐ 8 银行在上海路。
☐ 9 上海路离这里很远。
☐ 10 上海路在西边。
☐ 11 邮局在公园的前边。

Pronunciation

5 **Write pinyin for the words.**

1 哪儿 ______________
2 这儿 ______________
3 那儿 ______________
4 一点儿 ______________
5 一块儿 ______________
6 门口儿 ______________
7 北边儿 ______________

Now write sentences using the words given.

8 哪儿
____

9 这儿
____

10 那儿
____

LESSON 2

Objectives

1 **Vocabulary:** types of housing
2 **Reading:** understand an advertisement for a flat
3 **Writing:** describe a flat you want to live in
4 **Grammar:** express existence using 有
5 **Grammar:** ask questions using 有没有
6 **Grammar:** express location with the verb 在

Vocabulary

36

1 Number the words in the order you hear them.

- ☐ a 公寓
- ☐ b 房子
- ☐ c 房间
- ☐ d 宿舍
- ☐ e 平方米
- ☐ f 出租
- ☐ g 地铁站
- ☐ h 交通

Reading

37

2 Read the advertisement and complete the sentences.

1 房子在南京路 ______ 号 ______ 楼。

2 公寓不太大，有 __________。

3 公园在房子的 __________。

4 地铁站在房子的 __________。

5 买东西很方便，附近有 __________ 和 __________。

安家乐居网

公寓出租 搜索

公寓出租

南京路28号5楼，80平方米，有两个房间。房子北边有公园，南边是购物中心。往西边走八分钟是地铁站，地铁站附近有超市，也有电影院。交通和买东西都很方便。

每月 ¥3200 电话：12928063715

联系人：王先生

Writing

3 Write a paragraph about the kind of flat you would like to live in.

____

____

____

____

____

____

____

Grammar

4 Put the words in the correct order to make sentences.

wǒ méiyǒu de fángzi chúfáng
1 我 / 没有 / 的 / 房子 / 厨房 /。

____

yǒu dōngbian yīyuàn de xuéxiào
2 有 / 东边 / 医院 / 的 / 学校 /。

____

chāoshì qiánbian gōngyuán yǒu
3 超市 / 前边 / 公园 / 有 /。

____

yínháng méiyǒu hòubian yóujú
4 银行 / 没有 / 后边 / 邮局 /。

____

méiyǒu gòuwù zhōngxīn fùjìn diànyǐngyuàn
5 没有 / 购物 中心 / 附近 / 电影院 /。

____

5 Write questions for the answers using 有没有.

Xuéxiào fùjìn yǒu shūdiàn
1 学校 附近 有 书店。

____

Gōngyuán nánbian yǒu fànguǎn
2 公园 南边 有 饭馆。

____

Diànyǐngyuàn hòubian méiyǒu yínháng
3 电影院 后边 没有 银行。

____

Yīyuàn de fùjìn méiyǒu chāoshì
4 医院 的 附近 没有 超市。

____

Dìtiě zhàn méiyǒu xǐshǒujiān
5 地铁 站 没有 洗手间。

____

6 Write five sentences about the location of the places on the map using 在.

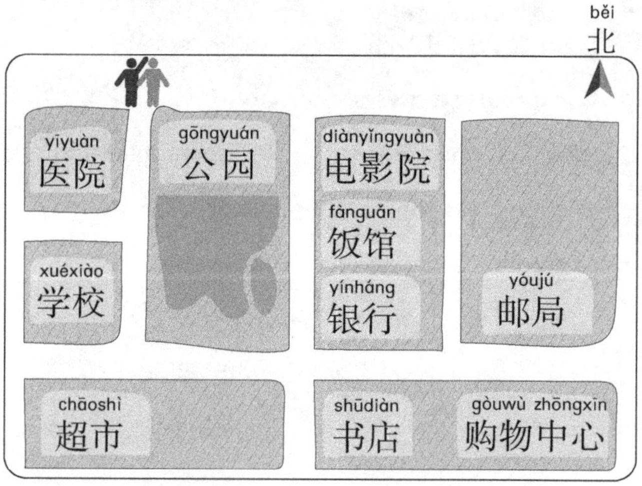

1 ______________________________

2 ______________________________

3 ______________________________

4 ______________________________

5 ______________________________

Now rewrite the sentences using 有 or 在.

Diànyǐngyuàn zài gōngyuán dōngbian
6 电影院 在 公园 东边。

Gōngyuán
公园 ______________________________。

Yīyuàn fùjìn méiyǒu yóujú
7 医院 附近 没有 邮局。

Yóujú
邮局 ______________________________。

Xuéxiào zài gōngyuán de xībian
8 学校 在 公园 的 西边。

Gōngyuán
公园 ______________________________。

Gòuwù zhōngxīn de běibian yǒu yóujú
9 购物 中心 的 北边 有 邮局。

yóujú
邮局 ______________________________。

LESSON 3

Objectives

1 **Reading:** understand descriptions of weekend activities

2 **Character reading:** recognise characters with the radicals 木 and 彳

3 **Character writing:** give directions

4 **Vocabulary extension:** places in the neighbourhood

Reading

38

1 Read Liu Li's email to her parents and check the true statements.

返回 回复 回复全部 转发 删除

爸爸、妈妈：

你们好吗？

我在大学认识了很多朋友。周末我们一起去吃中餐。我最喜欢去学校附近的饭馆，那里的菜很好吃，价钱也不贵。

星期天，我跟朋友去超市买东西。超市离大学很近，走十分钟左右，很方便。

刘丽

☐ 1 刘丽有很多朋友。

☐ 2 她喜欢跟朋友一起吃中餐。

☐ 3 学校附近饭馆的中餐很贵。

☐ 4 她跟朋友一起去超市。

☐ 5 超市离大学不远。

Character reading

2 Match the radicals with the meanings.

1 木 — a step

2 彳 — b tree

Now match the words with the meanings.

3 怎么样 — c lawyer

4 很 — d woods

5 林 — e how about

6 律师 — f very

Character writing

3 Make sentences using the words given.

1 楼　　附近

____

2 银行　　往

____

Vocabulary extension

4 Complete the table with the words in the box.

shāngdiàn 商店　yàodiàn 药店　lǚguǎn 旅馆
jiànshēnfáng 健身房　jǐngchájú 警察局　kāfēidiàn 咖啡店

Activities	Places
zhù 住 (live)	
hē kāfēi 喝 咖啡 (drink coffee)	
mǎi dōngxi 买 东西 (shopping)	
zuò yùndòng 做 运动 (exercise)	
qiúzhù 求助 (get help)	

CHARACTER WRITING

Objectives

1 Practise five characters with the radicals 木 and 彳

2 Learn to write nine common words for directions and types of student housing

1 Write the words containing the radicals 木 and 彳.

hěn *very*

很

yínháng *bank*

银

行

wǎng *towards*

往

lóu *building, storey*

楼

shǒujī *mobile phone*

手

机

2 Write the characters following the correct stroke order.

dōngbian *east*

东

边

nán *south*

南 南 南 南 南 南 南 南 南

南

xī *west*

西 西 西 西 西 西

西

běi *north*

北 北 北 北 北

北

qián *front*

前 前 前 前 前 前 前 前 前

前

hòu *back*

后 后 后 后 后 后

后

fùjìn *vicinity, nearby*

附 附 附 附 附 附 附

附

近 近 近 近 近 近 近

近

fáng *house*

房 房 房 房 房 房 房 房

房

sùshè *dormitory*

宿 宿 宿 宿 宿 宿 宿 宿 宿 宿 宿

宿

舍 舍 舍 舍 舍 舍 舍 舍

舍

SELF-ASSESSMENT

Complete the checklist, using the criteria below.

1 = I need a lot of help to do this.

2 = I can do this with a little help.

3 = I can do this fairly well.

4 = I can do this very well.

5 = I can do this almost perfectly.

LANGUAGE SKILL	PROGRESS	YOUR SCORE
PRONUNCIATION	• I can identify and say words with retroflex "r".	
VOCABULARY	• I can give directions and describe locations. • I can name five places in a neighbourhood and three types of student housing.	
GRAMMAR	• I can express existence using 有. • I can ask questions using 有没有. • I can express location with the verb 在.	
LISTENING	• I can identify locations of and directions to places. • I can understand people describing locations and giving directions.	
READING	• I know the meanings of the radicals 木 and 亻. • I can recognise characters in advertisements for houses or flats. • I can understand descriptions of weekend activities.	
SPEAKING	• I can describe locations. • I can ask for and give directions.	
WRITING	• I can write five characters with the radicals 木 and 亻, and nine common words for directions and types of housing. • I can write a short description about my ideal flat.	

UNIT 10 Zuò huǒchē ba 坐火车吧。

Let's take the train.

LESSON | 1

Objectives

1 **Vocabulary:** means of transport

2 **Conversation and listening:** understand transport options

3 **Conversation and listening:** make an appointment

4 **Pronunciation:** difference between "q" and "ch"

Vocabulary

1 Find six means of transport in the table.

dì 地	tiě 铁	yī 一	gōng 公	hǎi 海
chū 出	shàng 上	zhōng 中	gòng 共	yuè 月
zū 租	dà 大	qí 骑	qì 汽	fāng 方
chē 车	zì 自	xíng 行	chē 车	xué 学
yuán 园	huǒ 火	xīn 心	zhàn 站	yóu 由
zǒu 走	chē 车	fēi 飞	jī 机	chǎng 场

1 ______________ 4 ______________

2 ______________ 5 ______________

3 ______________ 6 ______________

Conversation and listening

2 Complete the conversation with the words in the box.

zuǒyòu 左右	háishi 还是	hěn yuǎn 很 远
fāngbiàn 方便	zěnme 怎么	zěnmeyàng 怎么样

永民：(1) __________ 去三里屯？坐地铁去 (2) __________？

安娜：地铁站 (3) __________，坐地铁不太 (4) __________。

永民：坐出租车 (5) __________ 公共 汽车？

安娜：坐出租车吧。十五分钟 (6) __________，也不太贵。

永民：好吧。

39

Now listen to the conversation and answer the questions.

7 永民要去哪里?

____

8 他坐地铁去吗?

____

9 附近有没有地铁站?

____

10 他坐什么车去?

____

11 这里离三里屯远吗? 坐出租车要多少分钟?

____

40

3 Listen to the conversation and check the true statements.

A: 这个星期你有时间吗? 我们一起吃饭。

B: 我明天有时间。

A: 好。明天几点?

B: 晚上七点,可以吗?

A: 没问题。你喜欢中餐还是日本菜?

B: 吃中餐吧。我星期六吃了日本菜。

A: 我们去"北京厨房",好不好?

B: 好。明天七点在餐厅门口见。

☐ 1 他们明天一起吃饭。

☐ 2 他们七点到餐厅。

☐ 3 她不喜欢吃中餐,她要吃日本菜。

Pronunciation

41

4 Check the correct pinyin for the words.

1	一起	☐ a yīchǐ	☐ b yìqǐ
2	裙子	☐ a qúnzi	☐ b chúnzi
3	请问	☐ a chénwèn	☐ b qǐngwèn
4	价钱	☐ a jiàqián	☐ b jiàchén
5	骑车	☐ a chí chē	☐ b qí chē
6	前边	☐ a qiánbian	☐ b chēbian
7	吃饭	☐ a qīfàn	☐ b chīfàn
8	出租车	☐ a chūzūchē	☐ b qūzūchē
9	唱歌	☐ a chànggē	☐ b qiànggē
10	超市	☐ a qiāoshì	☐ b chāoshì
11	厨房	☐ a qúfáng	☐ b chúfáng
12	船	☐ a chuán	☐ b quán

Now listen and check your answers. Then write sentences using the words given.

13 一起 骑车

____

14 请问 前边

____

15 出租车 超市

____

LESSON | 2

Objectives

1 **Vocabulary:** holiday activities

2 **Reading:** understand people making travel plans

3 **Writing:** describe one's travel plans and make an invitation

4 **Grammar:** alternative questions with 还是

5 **Grammar:** questions ending with 好吗

6 **Grammar:** express superlatives with 最

7 **Grammar:** use the particle 吧

Vocabulary

1 Match the words with the meanings.

1 坐 船 (zuò chuán)	a take photos
2 游览 (yóulǎn)	b go sightseeing
3 爬山 (páshān)	c climb a mountain
4 拍照 (pāizhào)	d visit a scenic site
5 参观 景点 (cānguān jǐngdiǎn)	e take a boat

Reading

42

2 Read Yeong-min's online conversation with Mark, and answer the questions.

1 永民和马克暑假要做什么?

____

2 他们计划去哪里旅行?

____

3 他们要坐船游览吗?

____

4 他们怎么去桂林? 几月去?

____

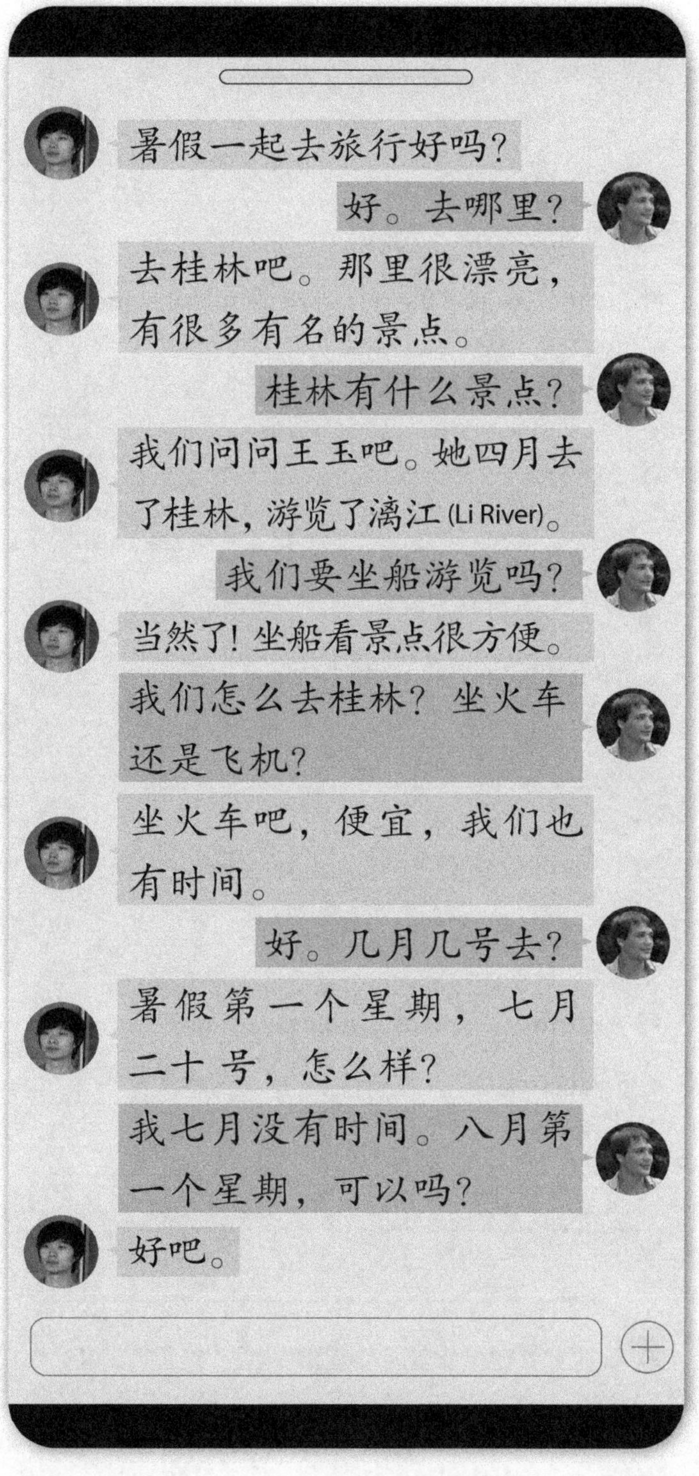

Writing

3 **Write an email to a friend, telling him/her your travel plans for the summer vacation. Invite him/her to go with you.**

____

____

____

Grammar

4 **Put the words in the correct order to make questions.**

1. háishi / nǐ / yào / qúnzi / kùzi
还是 / 你 / 要 / 裙子 / 裤子 /?

____

2. nǐ / xǐhuan / chī / háishi / Rìběncài / Yìdàlìcài
你 / 喜欢 / 吃 / 还是 / 日本菜 / 意大利菜 / ?

____

3. háishi / sān diǎn / dǎ lánqiú / sì diǎn
还是 / 三 点 / 打 篮球 / 四 点 /?

____

4. nǐ / háishi / jīntiān / yǒu shíjiān / míngtiān
你 / 还是 / 今天 / 有 时间 / 明天 /?

____

5 **Write the questions in Chinese using 好吗.**

1. Shall we have Chinese food?

____

2. Shall we take a taxi?

____

3. Shall we go to see a movie on Friday evening?

____

6 **Answer the questions using 最.**

1. Nǐ zuì xǐhuan xīngqījǐ
你 最 喜欢 星期几?

____

2. Shénme yánsè zuì piàoliang
什么 颜色 最 漂亮?

____

3. Shénme zuì hǎochī
什么 最 好吃?

____

4. Nǐ zuì xǐhuan shéi
你 最 喜欢 谁?

____

7 **Translate the sentences into English.**

1. Nǐ shìshi ba
你 试试 吧。

____

2. Wǒmen qù tīng yīnyuèhuì ba
我们 去 听 音乐会 吧。

____

3. Piányi yīdiǎnr ba
便宜 一点儿 吧。

____

4. Jīntiān chī Rìběncài ba
今天 吃 日本菜 吧。

____

5. Xīngqī'èr qù kàn diànyǐng ba
星期二 去 看 电影 吧。

____

6. Zuò dìtiě ba, dìtiě fāngbiàn yīdiǎnr
坐 地铁 吧，地铁 方便 一点儿。

____

LESSON 3

Objectives

1 **Conversation and listening:** understand dinner plans
2 **Character reading:** recognise characters with the radicals 又 and 饣
3 **Character writing:** make appointments
4 **Vocabulary extension:** places related to transport

Conversation and listening

43

1 Listen to the conversation and check the true statements.

史蒂夫：美国银行前边有个意大利餐厅，你知道吗？
永民：当然知道！那个意大利餐厅很有名。
史蒂夫：我们去那里吃饭，好吗？
永民：太好了！我最喜欢意大利菜。我们明天去吧。
史蒂夫：我请两个朋友一起去，可以吗？
永民：没问题。
史蒂夫：我给朋友们打电话，请他们明天晚上七点到餐厅门口。
永民：好。

☐ 1 史蒂夫和永民今天吃意大利菜。
☐ 2 这个餐厅不太有名。
☐ 3 餐厅离美国银行不远。
☐ 4 他们要跟朋友一起吃意大利菜。
☐ 5 他们明天晚上六点在餐厅门口见。

Character reading

2 Match the radicals with the meanings.

1 又	a eat
2 饣	b again

Now match the words with the meanings.

3 朋友	c hair
4 参观	d dinner
5 头发	e friend
6 晚饭	f visit

Character writing

3 Make sentences using the words given.

1 参观　景点

____

2 饭馆　门口

____

Vocabulary extension

4 Write sentences using the words given.

1 飞机场　火车站

____

2 停车场　加油站

____

CHARACTER WRITING

Objectives

1 Practise seven characters with the radicals 又 and 饣

2 Learn to write six common words for modes of transport and holiday activities

1 Write the words containing the radicals 又 and 饣.

xǐhuan *like*

喜 喜 喜 喜 喜 喜 喜 喜 喜 喜 喜 喜

喜

欢 欢 欢 欢 欢 欢

欢

tóufa *hair*

头 头 头 头 头

头

发 发 发 发 发

发

duì *right, correct*

对 对 对 对 对

对

péngyou *friend*

朋 朋 朋 朋 朋 朋 朋 朋

朋

友 友 友 友

友

shuāng *pair*

双 双 双 双

双

fànguǎn *restaurant*

饭 饭 饭 饭 饭 饭 饭

饭

馆 馆 馆 馆 馆 馆 馆 馆 馆 馆 馆

馆

2 **Write the words following the correct stroke order.**

huǒchē *train*

火

车

lǚxíng *travel*

旅

行

páshān *climb a mountain*

爬

山

cānguān *visit (a place)*

参

观

pāizhào *take photos*

拍

照

chuán *boat*

船

SELF-ASSESSMENT

Complete the checklist, using the criteria below.

1 = I need a lot of help to do this.
2 = I can do this with a little help.
3 = I can do this fairly well.
4 = I can do this very well.
5 = I can do this almost perfectly.

LANGUAGE SKILL	PROGRESS	YOUR SCORE
PRONUNCIATION	• I can identify and say words with the initials "q" and "ch".	
VOCABULARY	• I can name five types of transport. • I know the words used to make plans and appointments. • I know five words for holiday activities.	
GRAMMAR	• I can ask alternative questions with 还是. • I can make a suggestion or ask for an opinion using 好吗. • I can express superlatives with 最. • I can use the particle 吧 to express commands or suggestions.	
LISTENING	• I can understand descriptions of different types of transport. • I can understand people talking about appointments and simple plans.	
READING	• I know the meanings of the radicals 又 and 饣. • I can recognise characters to understand simple travel plans and invitations.	
SPEAKING	• I can talk about different types of transport. • I can discuss which type of transport to take. • I can describe and make simple plans.	
WRITING	• I can write seven characters with the radicals 又 and 饣, and six common words for modes of transport and holiday activities. • I can write simple travel plans and invitations.	

UNIT 11 Wǒ huì tiàowǔ
我会跳舞。

I can dance.

LESSON 1

Objectives

1 **Vocabulary:** types of sport, likes and dislikes

2 **Conversation and listening:** talk about sports and make appointments

3 **Conversation and listening:** talk about a football match and a favourite player

4 **Pronunciation:** difference between "zh" and "ch"

Vocabulary

1 Write the sports in Chinese.

1 tennis ____________________

2 table tennis ____________________

3 football ____________________

4 swimming ____________________

5 basketball ____________________

6 dancing ____________________

Now complete the sentences with the words above.

7 我 喜欢 ________，不 喜欢 ________。
(Wǒ xǐhuan … bù xǐhuan)

8 我 的 朋友 喜欢 ________，不 喜欢 ________。
(Wǒ de péngyou xǐhuan … bù xǐhuan)

Conversation and listening

2 Complete the conversation with the words in the box.

zěnmeyàng 怎么样	wǎngqiú bǐsài 网球 比赛	ménkǒu 门口
huì bú huì 会不会	yǒu shíjiān 有 时间	xǐhuan 喜欢

永民：星期天下午去看 (1) ________ 好吗？

安娜：好！我 (2) ________ 看网球比赛。

永民：你 (3) ________ 打网球？

安娜：当然会，我打网球很不错。

永民：(4) ________ 我们一起去打网球吧。

安娜：好。下个星期二下午你有时间吗？
我们去体育场打网球 (5) ________？

永民：我有时间。我们三点在体育场
(6) ________ 见，好吗？

安娜：没问题。

44 Now listen to the conversation and check the true statements.

- ☐ 7 永民和安娜喜欢看网球比赛。
- ☐ 8 他们星期日去看比赛。
- ☐ 9 他们不会打网球。
- ☐ 10 他们星期二下午去体育场。

45 **3** Listen to the conversation and check the true statements.

永民：马克，星期二的足球比赛，哪个球队赢了？
马克：当然是英格兰队赢了！
永民：我真希望是法国队赢！
马克：法国队不错，但是我喜欢英格兰队。
永民：你最喜欢哪个运动员？
马克：我最喜欢英格兰队的David。

- ☐ 1 马克昨天看了足球比赛。
- ☐ 2 昨天是英格兰队赢。
- ☐ 3 马克和永民都希望英格兰队赢。
- ☐ 4 马克不喜欢英格兰队的运动员。

Pronunciation

46 **4** Check the correct initial for the characters.

	zh	ch
1 吃	a ☐	b ☐
2 出	a ☐	b ☐
3 唱	a ☐	b ☐
4 住	a ☐	b ☐
5 这	a ☐	b ☐
6 真	a ☐	b ☐
7 船	a ☐	b ☐
8 中	a ☐	b ☐

Now listen and check your answers. Then write pinyin for the words.

9 吃中餐 ________

10 超市 ________

11 冲浪 ________

12 城市 ________

13 知道 ________

14 分钟 ________

15 服装市场 ________

16 拍照 ________

LESSON 2

Objectives

1. **Vocabulary:** recreational activities, types of sports
2. **Reading:** understand a blog entry about sports
3. **Communication:** conduct a survey about sports
4. **Grammar:** use the modal verb 可以
5. **Grammar:** use the modal verb 会
6. **Grammar:** pivotal sentences
7. **Grammar:** talk about past actions with 过

Vocabulary

47

1 Number the sports in the order you hear them.

- ☐ a qiánshuǐ 潜水
- ☐ b lánqiú 篮球
- ☐ c chōnglàng 冲浪
- ☐ d pīngpāngqiú 乒乓球
- ☐ e bèngjí 蹦极
- ☐ f huáxuě 滑雪
- ☐ g wǎngqiú 网球
- ☐ h pǎobù 跑步

Reading

48

2 Complete the questionnaire with information from Yeong-min's blog.

wǒ de xiūxián yùndòng
我的休闲运动

我叫永民。今年十八岁。我是韩国人，现在住在北京大学附近的公寓。我喜欢跑步，每天早上跑三十分钟。每个星期三上午我跟朋友踢足球。每个星期五下午我跟史蒂夫在大学的体育场打篮球。我不喜欢在健身房做运动。我不会游泳，希望下个月开始学游泳。

学生运动和休闲问卷

姓名：

年龄：

性别：

国籍：

你喜欢什么运动？

踢足球 ☐ 冲浪 ☐

游泳 ☐ 滑雪 ☐

打篮球 ☐ 潜水 ☐

打乒乓球 ☐ 蹦极 ☐

其他 ☐

你每星期做多少个小时运动？

☐ 0 ☐ 1—2 ☐ 3—4 ☐ 5—10

你什么时候做运动？ ________

你和谁一起做运动？ ________

你在哪里做运动？

☐ 家里 ☐ 健身房 ☐ 体育场

Communication

3 Use the questionnaire in Activity 2 to conduct a survey on your classmates' recreational activities.

Now complete the sentences using your survey results.

Tóngxuémen zuì xǐhuan de yùndòng shì
1 同学们 最 喜欢 的 运动 是______
________。

Tóngxuémen zuì bù xǐhuan de yùndòng shì
2 同学们 最不 喜欢 的 运动 是____
________。

Tóngxuémen měi xīngqī zuì duō zuò gè
3 同学们 每 星期 最 多 做 ______ 个
xiǎoshí yùndòng
小时 运动。

Grammar

4 Write questions for the answers .

Nǐ shǔjià kěyǐ qù Guìlín lǚxíng
1 你 暑假 可以 去 桂林 旅行。

____

Nǐ kěyǐ gěi lǎoshī xiě diànzǐ yóujiàn
2 你 可以 给 老师 写 电子 邮件。

____

Nǐ kěyǐ lái wǒ de shēngrì pàiduì
3 你 可以 来 我 的 生日 派对。

____

5 Write the sentences in Chinese.

1 Can you swim?

____

2 We can't play basketball.

____

3 They can dance.

____

6 Put the words in the correct order to make sentences.

yīnyuèhuì Shǐdìfū Ānnà tīng qǐng
1 音乐会 / 史蒂夫 / 安娜 / 听 / 请 / 。

____

wǒ Yīnggélán duì yíng xīwàng
2 我 / 英格兰 队 / 赢 / 希望 / 。

____

chī Wáng lǎoshī qǐng Rìběncài wǒmen
3 吃 / 王 老师 / 请 / 日本菜 / 我们 / 。

____

qǐng tiàowǔ Wáng Yù Yǒngmín
4 请 / 跳舞 / 王 玉 / 永民 / 。

____

xīwàng péngyǒu tā dǎ diànhuà gěi tā
5 希望 / 朋友 / 他 / 打 电话 / 给 他 / 。

____

7 Put 过 in the correct places in the sentences.

Wǒ mèimei qù Jiānádà
1 我 妹妹 去 加拿大。

____

Mǎkè méi xué dǎ wǎngqiú
2 马克 没 学 打 网球。

____

Mǎ yīshēng de dìdi zuò jìzhě
3 马 医生 的 弟弟 做 记者。

____

Tāmen qù Běijīng Sānlǐtún
4 他们 去 北京 三里屯。

____

Wǒmen cānguān hěn duō jǐngdiǎn
5 我们 参观 很 多 景点。

____

LESSON | 3

Objectives

1 **Conversation:** talk about a recreational class
2 **Character reading:** recognise characters with the radicals 王 and 钅
3 **Character writing:** describe recreational activities
4 **Vocabulary extension:** different types of sport

Conversation

1 Match the questions with the answers.

1 什么时间？ ______
2 学跳舞多少钱？ ______
3 学校在哪里？ ______
4 我们一起学跳舞好吗？ ______

a 在北京大学的东边，购物中心的三楼。
b 每星期四晚上八点。
c 好，我喜欢跳舞。
d 一小时五十块。

Character reading

2 Match the radicals with the meanings.

1 王	a metal
2 钅	b jade

Now match the words with the meanings.

3 希望	c price
4 地铁	d sports team
5 球队	e subway
6 价钱	f hope

Character writing

3 Make sentences using the words given.

1 周末　足球

______

2 喜欢　游泳

______

Vocabulary extension

4 Answer the questions with the words in the box.

lánqiú 篮球	qūgùnqiú 曲棍球	wǎngqiú 网球	páiqiú 排球
bàngqiú 棒球	huáxuě 滑雪	bèngjí 蹦极	zúqiú 足球
chōnglàng 冲浪	gǎnlǎnqiú 橄榄球	qiánshuǐ 潜水	yóuyǒng 游泳
pǎobù 跑步	pīngpāngqiú 乒乓球		

Nǐ huì shénme yùndòng
1 你 会 什么 运动？

______

Nǐ xǐhuan shénme yùndòng
2 你 喜欢 什么 运动？

______

Nǐ xiǎng kàn shénme bǐsài
3 你 想 看 什么 比赛？

______

CHARACTER WRITING

Objectives

1 Practise six characters with the radicals 王 and 钅

2 Learn to write six common words for abilities and types of sport

1 Write the words containing the radicals 王 and 钅.

wán *play*

玩

xiànzài *now*

现 在

bān *measure word used for a flight*

班

zúqiú *football*

足 球

qián *money*

钱

dìtiě *subway*

地 铁

2 Write the words following the correct stroke order.

kěyǐ *can*

可

以

huì *can, be able to*

会

yóuyǒng *swim*

游

泳

wǎngqiú *tennis*

网

球

tī *play (with feet), kick*

踢

pīngpāng *table tennis*

乒

乓

SELF-ASSESSMENT

Complete the checklist, using the criteria below.

1 = I need a lot of help to do this.
2 = I can do this with a little help.
3 = I can do this fairly well.
4 = I can do this very well.
5 = I can do this almost perfectly.

LANGUAGE SKILL	PROGRESS	YOUR SCORE
PRONUNCIATION	• I can identify and say words with the initials "zh" and "ch".	
VOCABULARY	• I can name five types of sport. • I can name five different recreational activities.	
GRAMMAR	• I can use the modal verb 可以 to talk about ability, possibility and permission. • I can use the modal verb 会 to talk about the ability to do something. • I can use pivotal sentences to express an invitation or wish. • I can use the particle 过 to talk about past actions.	
LISTENING	• I can identify different sports and recreational activities in a conversation. • I can understand people's descriptions of the sports they like and dislike.	
READING	• I know the meanings of the radicals 王 and 钅. • I can understand simple questionnaires and blog entries about sports and recreational activities.	
SPEAKING	• I can talk about sports activities I like and dislike.	
WRITING	• I can write six characters with the radicals 王 and 钅, and six common words for abilities and sports. • I can describe my favourite sports and recreational activities. • I can complete a simple questionnaire about sports and recreational activities.	

UNIT 12 我们去看京剧。

Wǒmen qù kàn jīngjù

We're going to the Beijing opera.

LESSON 1

Objectives

1 **Vocabulary:** holiday activities

2 **Conversation and listening:** talk about holiday plans

3 **Pronunciation:** sentence intonation

4 **Grammar:** plans, past actions, alternatives, suggestions, times and abilities

Vocabulary

1 Match the words with the meanings.

1 huíjiā 回家	a go shopping
2 kàn jīngjù 看 京剧	b go back home
3 qù lǚxíng 去 旅行	c go to a concert
4 tīng yīnyuèhuì 听 音乐会	d go travelling
5 gòuwù 购物	e climb a mountain
6 páshān 爬山	f watch Beijing opera

Now write two sentences with some of the words above.

7 ______________________________

8 ______________________________

Conversation and listening

2 Put the sentences in the correct order to make a conversation.

a 我六月去过新加坡。那里很不错，有很好的购物中心，东西的价钱也不贵。

b 你去新加坡做什么？

c 安娜，这个假期你打算去什么地方旅行？

d 太好了！我喜欢购物。

e 十二月有我喜欢的音乐会，我想去听音乐会。

f 我打算去新加坡。

The correct order is ______________________.

49

Now listen to the conversation and answer the questions.

1 安娜假期打算去哪里？

____

2 什么时候有安娜喜欢的音乐会？

____

3 安娜想在那里做什么？

____

4 那里的购物中心怎么样？

____

5 永民去过新加坡吗？

____

Pronunciation

50

3 Mark the intonation for the sentences using ↑ (rising tone) and ↓ (falling tone).

Gēge jīntiān huíjiā ma
1 哥哥 今天 回家 吗？ ______

Bié qù Jiānádà le tài yuǎn le
2 别去加拿大了，太 远 了！ ______

Nǐ jiàqī dǎsuàn qù Rìběn ma
3 你 假期 打算 去 日本 吗？ ______

Wǒ yào gěi Ānnà xiě diànzǐ yóujiàn
4 我 要 给 安娜 写 电子 邮件。 ______

Wǒ zuò fēijī qù nǐ ne
5 我 坐 飞机 去，你 呢？ ______

Nǐ de gōngyù lí dàxué yuǎn ma
6 你 的 公寓 离 大学 远 吗？ ______

Wǒ jiějie xǐhuan chī zhōngcān
7 我 姐姐 喜欢 吃 中餐。 ______

Wǒ zhōumò qù kàn yéye nǎinai
8 我 周末 去 看 爷爷 奶奶。 ______

Now listen and check your answers.

Grammar

4 Translate the sentences into English.

Nǐ kàn guo jīngjù ma
1 你 看 过 京剧 吗？

____

Nǐ dǎsuàn zài Lúndūn zuò shénme
2 你 打算 在 伦敦 做 什么？

____

Nǐ xiǎng chī zhōngcān háishi Rìběncài
3 你 想 吃 中餐 还是 日本菜？

____

Nǐ shénme shíhou qù shūdiàn
4 你 什么 时候 去 书店？

____

Zhōumò yìqǐ qù kàn diànyǐng zěnmeyàng
5 周末 一起 去 看 电影，怎么样？

____

Zhège chāoshì de dōngxi hěn guì bié qù le
6 这个 超市 的 东西 很 贵，别 去 了。

____

Wǒmen yìqǐ qù lǚxíng hǎo ma
7 我们 一起 去 旅行，好 吗？

____

Bàba jǐ diǎn huíjiā
8 爸爸 几 点 回家？

____

Nǐ huì bú huì dǎ wǎngqiú
9 你 会 不 会 打 网球？

____

Wǒ Xīngqīliù mǎi le yì tiáo hóng qúnzi
10 我 星期六 买 了 一 条 红 裙子。

____

LESSON 2

Objectives

1 **Vocabulary:** cities in China and places of interest

2 **Grammar:** express alternatives using 或者

3 **Grammar:** express alternatives using 或者 and 还是

4 **Reading:** understand simple online chat messages about holiday plans

5 **Writing:** suggest a place to visit

6 **Grammar:** express regular events with 每……都……

Vocabulary

1 Write six words about cities and places of interest using the characters in the table.

lì 历	guǎng 广	xiāng 香	shǐ 史	bīng 兵
xī 西	mǎ 马	shàng 上	shì 市	cháng 长
hǎi 海	běi 北	ān 安	yǒng 俑	nián 年
gǎng 港	zhōu 州	chéng 城	qiān 千	jīng 京

1 ______________ 4 ______________

2 ______________ 5 ______________

3 ______________ 6 ______________

Grammar

2 Put the words in the correct order to make sentences.

1 nǐmen zuò qù dìtiě huòzhě gōnggòng qìchē
你们 / 坐 / 去 / 地铁 / 或者 / 公共汽车 / 。

____

2 Xīngqīyī huòzhě yéye kàn Xīngqīsān qù yīshēng
星期一 / 或者 / 爷爷 / 看 / 星期三 / 去 / 医生 / 。

____

3 yígè huòzhě tā yǒu gēge jiějie
一个 / 或者 / 他 / 有 / 哥哥 / 姐姐 / 。

____

4 Měiguórén huòzhě shì Jiānádàrén tāmen
美国人 / 或者 / 是 / 加拿大人 / 他们 / 。

____

3 Choose the correct words to complete the sentences.

1 Nǐ xǐhuan hēisè háishi huòzhě lánsè
你 喜欢 黑色 (还是 / 或者) 蓝色？

2 Jiàqī wǒ qù Měiguó háishi huòzhě Yīngguó lǚxíng
假期 我 去 美国 (还是 / 或者) 英国 旅行。

3 Shí diǎn háishi huòzhě shí diǎn bàn dōu kěyǐ
十 点 (还是 / 或者) 十 点 半 都 可以。

4 Tā shì lǎoshī háishi huòzhě xuésheng
她 是 老师 (还是 / 或者) 学生？

Reading

51

4 Read Yeong-min's online conversation with Steve and Mark.

暑假我打算跟朋友去英国或者澳大利亚旅行。两个地方我都没有去过。你们觉得哪个地方好玩？

英国不错！伦敦有很多有名的景点，购物的地方也很多。

我不太喜欢买东西。去景点的交通方便吗？

伦敦的地铁很方便，你也可以坐公共汽车或者出租车。

去澳大利亚吧。我有很多朋友在澳大利亚。你可以跟他们学潜水，很好玩。

好主意，我喜欢潜水！我应该去悉尼还是墨尔本呢？

去悉尼吧。那里的海很漂亮。

Now complete the sentences.

1 暑假永民打算跟 ______ 去旅行。

2 永民想去 ______ 或者 ______ 旅行。

3 史蒂夫说去 ______，那里有 ______ 和 ______。

4 在伦敦可以坐 ______，______，或者 ______ 游览景点。

5 马克说去 ______，在那里可以 ______。

Writing

5 Write a message to Yeong-min, suggesting a place to go and what he can do there.

____

____

____

____

Grammar

6 Rewrite the sentences using 每……都…….

1 Wǒ jīntiān xué Zhōngwén
我 今天 学 中文。

____

2 Xīngqīwǔ diànyǐngyuàn yǒu Měiguó diànyǐng
星期五 电影院 有 美国 电影。

____

3 Mǎkè gēn Wáng Yù zhōumò dǎ wǎngqiú
马克 跟 王 玉 周末 打 网球。

____

4 Xiānggǎng de dìtiězhàn yǒu yínháng
香港 的 地铁站 有 银行。

____

LESSON | 3

Objectives

1 **Conversation and listening:** talk about travel experiences
2 **Character reading:** recognise characters with the radicals ⺮ and 禾
3 **Character writing:** make plans for recreational activities
4 **Vocabulary extension:** holiday activities

Conversation and listening

52

1 Listen to the conversation and check the correct answers.

安娜： 永民，你去过中国哪几个城市？
永民： 我去过北京、上海和桂林。
安娜： 哪个城市最好玩？
永民： 每个城市都有很多景点，购物也很方便。三个地方都好玩。
安娜： 你最喜欢哪个城市？
永民： 我最喜欢桂林。

1 永民没去过什么城市？
☐ **a** 西安 ☐ **b** 北京 ☐ **c** 桂林

2 永民觉得哪个城市最好玩？
☐ **a** 北京 ☐ **b** 上海
☐ **c** 三个地方都好玩

3 他最喜欢哪个城市？
☐ **a** 北京 ☐ **b** 上海 ☐ **c** 桂林

Character reading

2 Match the radicals with the meanings.

1 ⺮ **a** grain
2 禾 **b** bamboo

Now match the words with the meanings.

3 出租车 **c** engineer
4 电子邮箱 **d** email inbox/address
5 打算 **e** taxi
6 工程师 **f** plan

Character writing

3 Make sentences using the words given.

1 打算 意大利

______

2 和 篮球

______

Vocabulary extension

4 Write four sentences using the words in the box.

dǎgōng 打工	zuò zhìyuànzhě 做 志愿者
shíxí 实习	yěyíng 野营

1 ______
2 ______
3 ______
4 ______

CHARACTER WRITING

Objectives

1. Practise five characters with the radicals ⺮ and 禾
2. Learn to write six common words for places and holiday activities

1 Write the words containing the radicals ⺮ and 禾.

dǎsuàn *plan*

打

算

lánqiú *basketball*

篮

球

hé *and*

和

zū *rent*

租

Xiānggǎng *Hong Kong*

香

港

2 Write the words following the correct stroke order.

dìfang *place*

地

方

chéngshì *city*

城

市

Xī'ān *Xi'an*

西

安

hǎowán *fun*

好

玩

lìshǐ *history*

历

史

zhǔyi *idea*

主

意

SELF-ASSESSMENT

Complete the checklist, using the criteria below.

1 = I need a lot of help to do this.
2 = I can do this with a little help.
3 = I can do this fairly well.
4 = I can do this really well.
5 = I can do this almost perfectly.

LANGUAGE SKILL	PROGRESS	YOUR SCORE
PRONUNCIATION	• I can say sentences with the correct intonation.	
VOCABULARY	• I can say the names of five cities in China. • I can name five holiday activities. • I know common words and phrases used to describe holiday plans and activities.	
GRAMMAR	• I can use 或者 and 还是 to express alternatives. • I can use 每……都…… to express regular events.	
LISTENING	• I can identify people's holiday preferences. • I can understand people talking about holiday plans.	
READING	• I know the meanings of the radicals ⺮ and 禾. • I can recognise the characters to understand chat messages about holiday plans.	
SPEAKING	• I can ask and answer questions about holiday plans. • I can express preferences for holiday plans.	
WRITING	• I can write five characters with the radicals ⺮ and 禾, and six common words for places and holiday activities. • I can suggest a place to visit and the things to do there.	

MY NOTES

MY NOTES

MY NOTES

MY NOTES

MY NOTES

Macmillan Education Limited
4 Crinan Street
London N1 9XW

Companies and representatives throughout the world

Multi-media pack ISBN 9781035120383

Published by arrangement with Macmillan Publishers (China) Limited

This edition published 2023
First edition published 2010

Publishers: Emma Bourne, Wang Fang
Project management: Cauvis Fung, Ivy Wang, Yang Piao
Author: Betty Hung
Academic advisors: Simon Greenall, Huang Dian, C. K. Tang
Editors: Wang Jianling, Yan Lina, Thomas McGrenery, Ivy Wang, Yang Diao

Audio materials produced by Sky Productions and DoubleDouble Creative & Production

Original design and page make-up by Beijing Fengshang Design Co. Ltd
Cover design by AM Design

The authors and publishers would like to thank the following for permission to reproduce their artwork/photographic material:
Tuweimei: pp19 (a-c, e-h), 21 (t, b), 35, 39, 44, 52, 71; Imagemore: p21 (m); VCG: p19 (d), p67 (a-e)

Cover photographs by VCG

We would also like to thank the following reviewers and teachers for their valuable and insightful comments:
Huang Dian (Senior lecturer in Chinese at the University of Westminster and Chair of the British Chinese Language Teaching Society), Dr. Song Lianyi (Principal Teaching Fellow in Chinese, China & Inner Asia Department, School of Oriental and African Studies, University of London), Ruby Costea (Supervisor for Elementary Foreign Language Instructors Johns Hopkins University Center for Talented Youth).

Printed and bound by CPI Group (UK) Ltd, Croydon CR0 4YY

POD 2025